THE BIGGEST STORY

CURRICULUM

VOLUME 6

COLORING & ACTIVITY BOOK

∷ CROSSWAY

WHEATON, ILLINOIS

The Biggest Story Curriculum, Volume 6

Copyright © 2023 by Crossway

Published by Crossway
    1300 Crescent Street
    Wheaton, Illinois 60187

Volume 6 of 6: Coloring & Activity Book

Original artwork by Don Clark for Invisible Creature, Inc.

Activity sheet content and artwork interpretation by Caleb Faires

First Printing 2023

Printed in China

ISBN: 978-1-4335-8903-4

Library of Congress Control Number: 2022946316

Crossway is a publishing ministry of Good News Publishers

RRDS		31	30	29	28	27	26	25	24	23
15	14	13	12	11	10	9	8	7	6	5	4	3	2	1

How to Use This Book

These worksheets give kids fresh ways to engage with and review each of the 104 Bible lessons from *The Biggest Story Curriculum*. Each fun activity page encourages children to recap the Big Truth and Memory Verse from the story, helping them apply what they have learned throughout the week, and the coloring pages give them a creative way to meditate on the story.

All of the coloring pages and activity sheets contained in this volume are available as free PDF downloads at TheBiggestStory.com, and teachers are encouraged to print and distribute as many copies as needed. Alternatively, teachers may choose to purchase additional copies of this volume to distribute to each child in the class.

A Note on Artwork

Users will notice that some stories within *The Biggest Story Curriculum* include pictures of Jesus. The illustration style shows that these are not meant to be depictions of Jesus as he really was on earth. Instead, the artwork used here recognizes that Jesus is indeed the main character of the Biggest Story.

And So It Begins

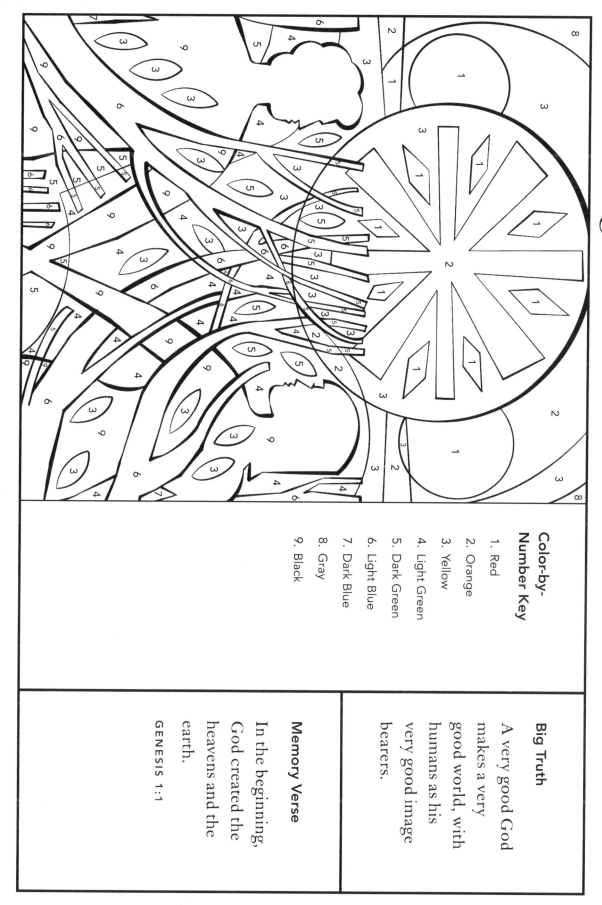

Color-by-Number Key

1. Red
2. Orange
3. Yellow
4. Light Green
5. Dark Green
6. Light Blue
7. Dark Blue
8. Gray
9. Black

Big Truth

A very good God makes a very good world, with humans as his very good image bearers.

Memory Verse

In the beginning, God created the heavens and the earth.

GENESIS 1:1

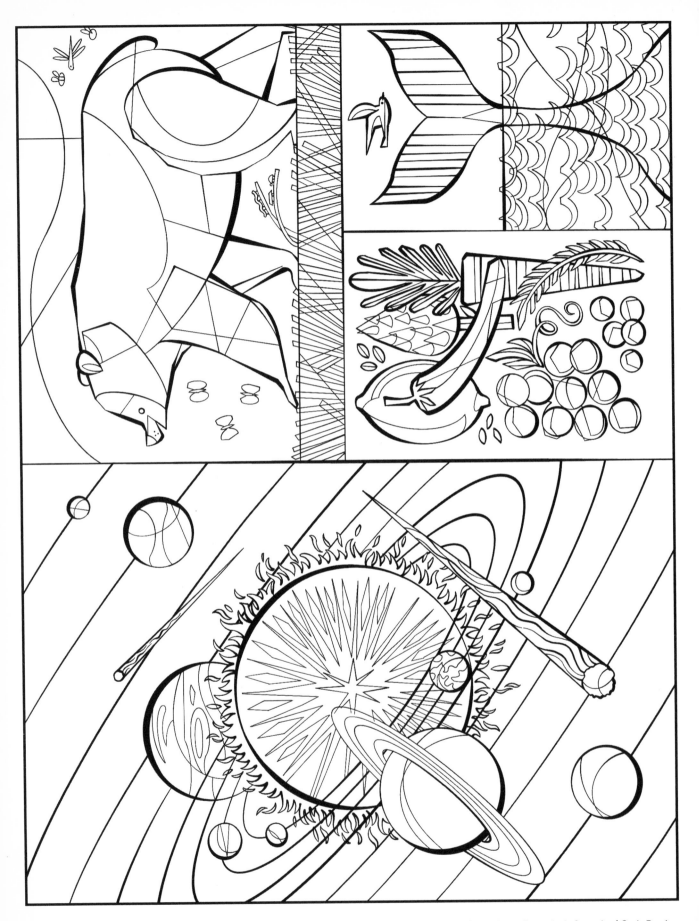

A Very Bad Day

From Genesis 3 and Romans 5 (ESV)

Across

4. "_____ are you above all the livestock"

5. The _____ was more crafty than any other beast

6. The _____ saw that the tree was good for food

7. "The serpent _____ me and I ate"

9. "She gave me the _____ of the tree and I ate"

Down

1. "He shall _____ your head"

2. "You will not surely _____"

3. God made for _____ and for his wife garments of skin

5. While we were still _____, Christ died for us

8. "I will put _____ between you and the woman"

Big Truth

Sin, suffering, and death came into the world because Adam disobeyed God.

Memory Verse

I will put enmity between you and the woman, and between your offspring and her offspring; he shall bruise your head, and you shall bruise his heel.

GENESIS 3:15

From Bad to Worse

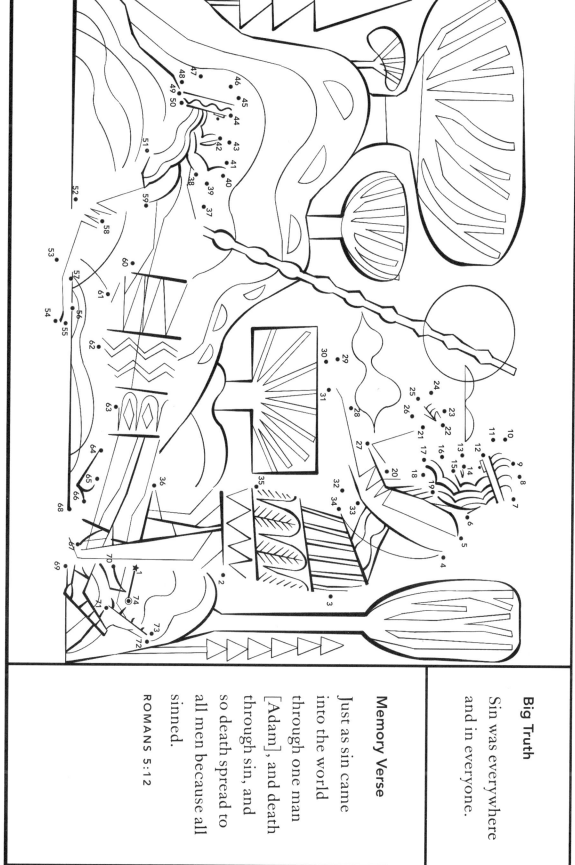

Big Truth

Sin was everywhere and in everyone.

Memory Verse

Just as sin came into the world through one man [Adam], and death through sin, and so death spread to all men because all sinned.

ROMANS 5:12

Rain, Rain, Go Away

START

FINISH

Big Truth

God sent a flood to judge all the wickedness on earth.

Memory Verse

Rain fell upon the earth forty days and forty nights.

GENESIS 7:12

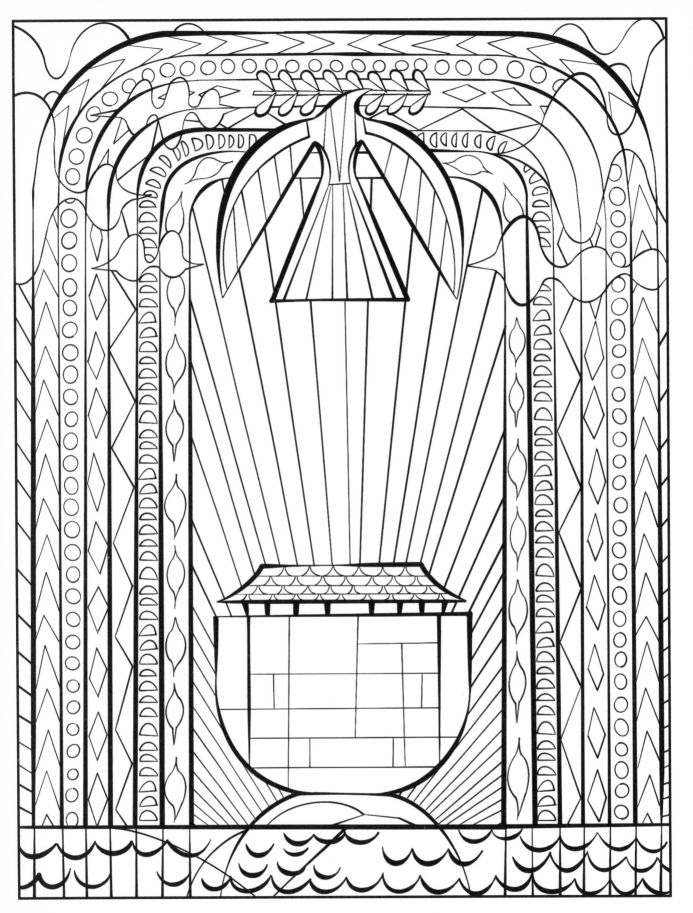

Story 4 • Genesis 6–9 • Rain, Rain, Go Away

A Table and a Tower

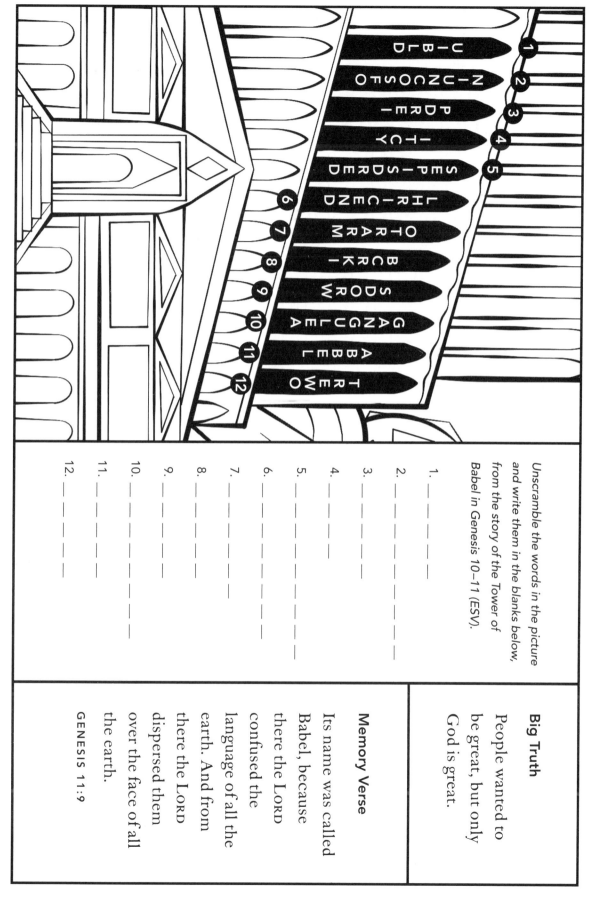

Unscramble the words in the picture and write them in the blanks below, from the story of the Tower of Babel in Genesis 10–11 (ESV).

1. _ _ _ _
2. _ _ _ _
3. _ _ _ _ _ _
4. _ _ _ _
5. _ _ _ _ _ _
6. _ _ _ _ _
7. _ _ _ _ _
8. _ _ _ _ _
9. _ _ _ _
10. _ _ _ _ _ _ _
11. _ _ _ _
12. _ _ _ _ _

Big Truth

People wanted to be great, but only God is great.

Memory Verse

Its name was called Babel, because there the LORD confused the language of all the earth. And from there the LORD dispersed them over the face of all the earth.

GENESIS 11:9

The Father of Nations

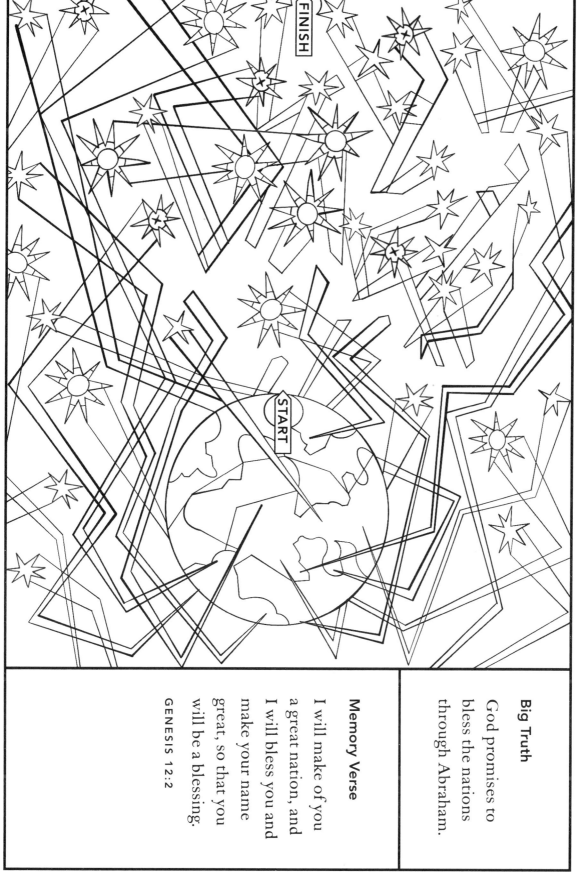

FINISH

START

Big Truth

God promises to bless the nations through Abraham.

Memory Verse

I will make of you a great nation, and I will bless you and make your name great, so that you will be a blessing.

GENESIS 12:2

Let's Make a Deal

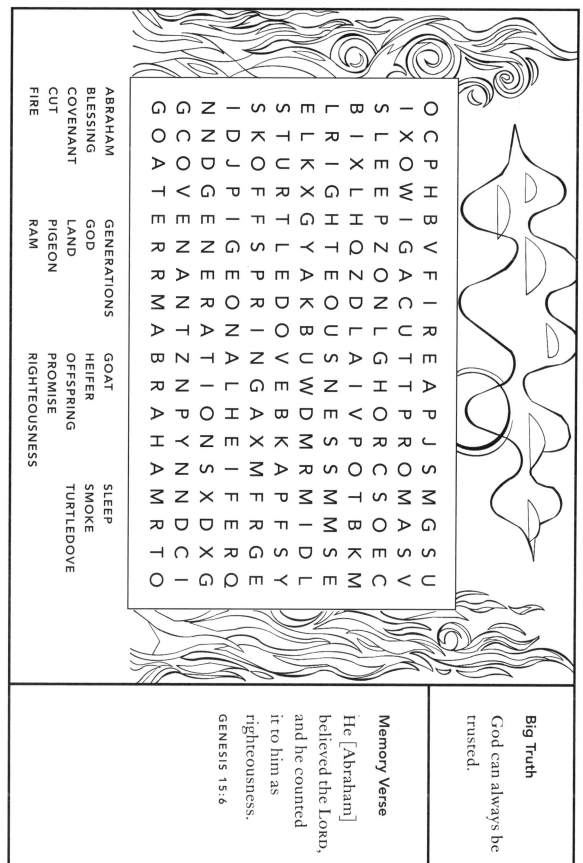

```
O  C  P  H  B  V  F  I  R  E  A  P  J  S  M  G  S  U
I  X  O  W  I  G  A  C  U  T  P  R  O  M  A  S  V
S  L  E  E  P  Z  O  N  L  G  H  O  R  C  S  O  E  C
B  I  X  L  H  Q  Z  D  L  A  I  V  P  O  T  B  K  M
L  R  I  G  H  T  E  O  U  S  N  E  S  S  M  M  S  E
E  L  K  X  G  Y  A  K  B  U  W  D  M  R  M  I  D  L
S  T  U  R  T  L  E  D  O  V  E  B  K  A  P  F  S  Y
S  K  O  F  S  P  R  I  N  G  A  X  M  F  R  G  E  O
I  D  J  P  I  G  E  O  N  A  L  H  E  I  F  E  R  Q
N  N  D  G  E  N  E  R  A  T  I  O  N  S  X  D  X  G
G  C  O  V  E  N  A  N  T  Z  N  P  Y  N  N  D  C  I
G  O  A  T  E  R  R  M  A  B  R  A  H  A  M  R  T  O
```

ABRAHAM	GENERATIONS	SLEEP
BLESSING	GOD	SMOKE
COVENANT	GOAT	TURTLEDOVE
CUT	HEIFER	
FIRE	LAND	
	OFFSPRING	
	PIGEON	
	PROMISE	
	RAM	
	RIGHTEOUSNESS	

Big Truth

God can always be trusted.

Memory Verse

He [Abraham] believed the LORD, and he counted it to him as righteousness.

GENESIS 15:6

The Judge Judges Justly

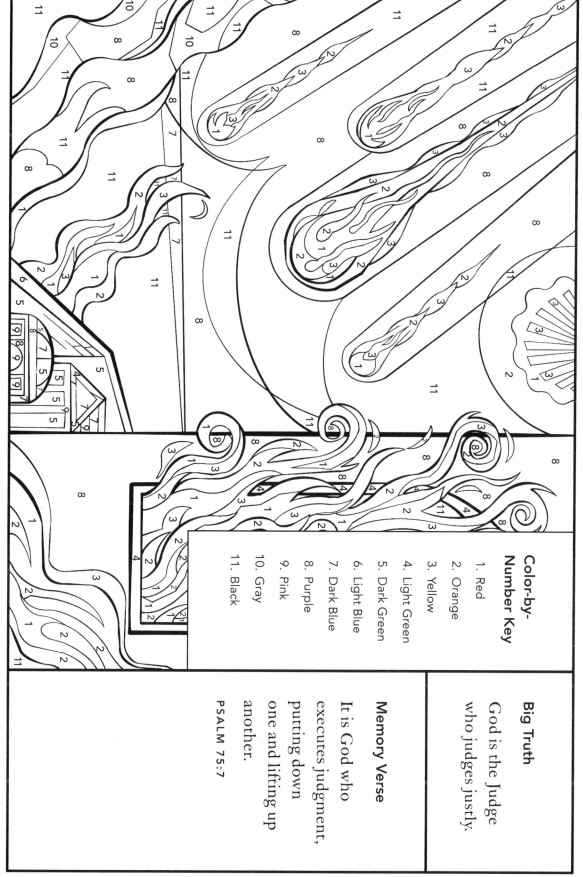

Color-by-Number Key

1. Red
2. Orange
3. Yellow
4. Light Green
5. Dark Green
6. Light Blue
7. Dark Blue
8. Purple
9. Pink
10. Gray
11. Black

Big Truth

God is the Judge who judges justly.

Memory Verse

It is God who executes judgment, putting down one and lifting up another.

PSALM 75:7

Story 8 • Genesis 18–19 • The Judge Judges Justly

It's a Boy!

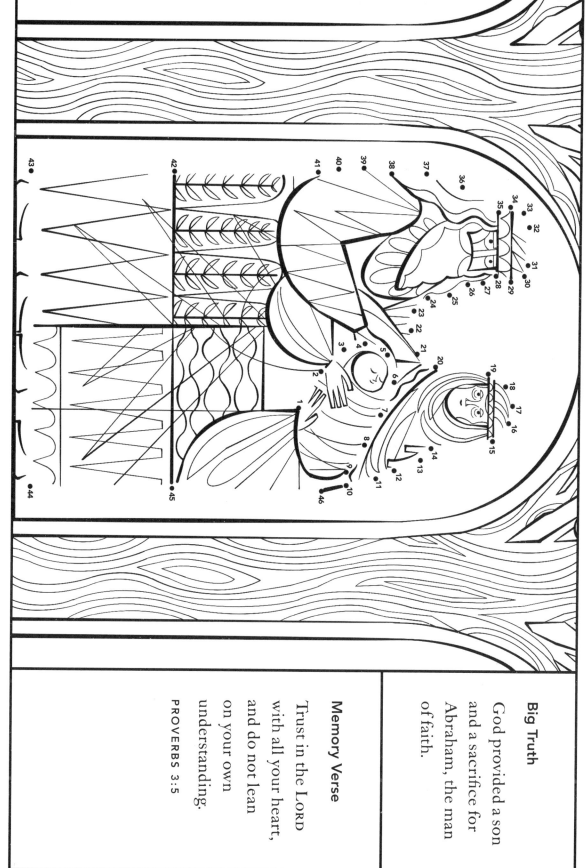

Big Truth

God provided a son and a sacrifice for Abraham, the man of faith.

Memory Verse

Trust in the LORD with all your heart, and do not lean on your own understanding.

PROVERBS 3:5

God's Tricky, Hairy, Blessed People

Unscramble the words below, from the story of Jacob and Esau in Genesis 25 and 27 (ESV).

BOJCA _____

UASE _____

KEHABRE _____

CAISA _____

AIHYR _____

MHOOST _____

SWINT _____

RTHHIGTIBR _____

SGLIBSNE _____

NEHUTR _____

NTSET _____

ETSW _____

DOLS _____

ADTEECH _____

Big Truth

God blesses his people even when they keep getting things wrong.

Memory Verse

Two nations are in your womb, and two peoples from within you shall be divided; the one shall be stronger than the other, the older shall serve the younger.

GENESIS 25:23

Story 10 • Genesis 25; 27 • God's Tricky, Hairy, Blessed People

Blessings in the Night

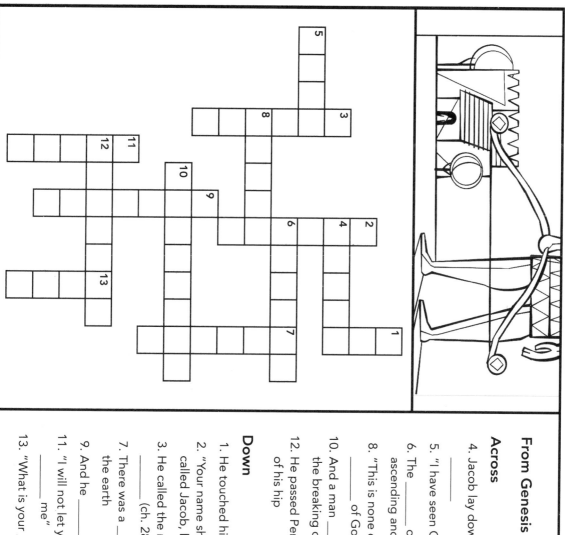

From Genesis 28 and 32 (ESV)

Across

4. Jacob lay down in that place to
   _____

5. "I have seen God face to _____
   _____"

6. The _____ of God were
   ascending and descending on it

8. "This is none other than the
   _____ of God"

10. And a man _____ with him until
    the breaking of the day

12. He passed Penuel, _____ because
    of his hip

Down

1. He touched his _____ socket

2. "Your name shall no longer be
   called Jacob, but _____"

3. He called the name of that place
   _____ (ch. 28)

7. There was a _____ set up on
   the earth

9. And he _____, and behold

11. "I will not let you go unless you
    _____ me"

13. "What is your _____ ?"

Big Truth

God reminds Jacob
that he will keep
his promise and
that he will be
with him.

Memory Verse

Behold, I am with
you and will keep
you wherever you
go, and will bring
you back to this
land. For I will not
leave you until I
have done what I
have promised you.

GENESIS 28:15

Joseph's Mean Brothers and What God Meant to Do

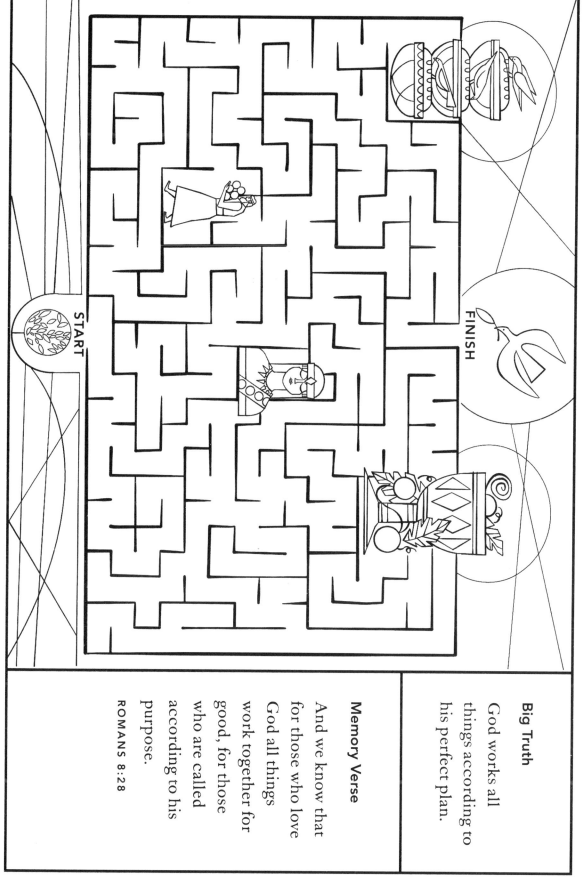

START

FINISH

Big Truth

God works all things according to his perfect plan.

Memory Verse

And we know that for those who love God all things work together for good, for those who are called according to his purpose.

ROMANS 8:28

Story 12 • Genesis 37; 50 • Joseph's Mean Brothers and What God Meant to Do

God Raises Up a Deliverer

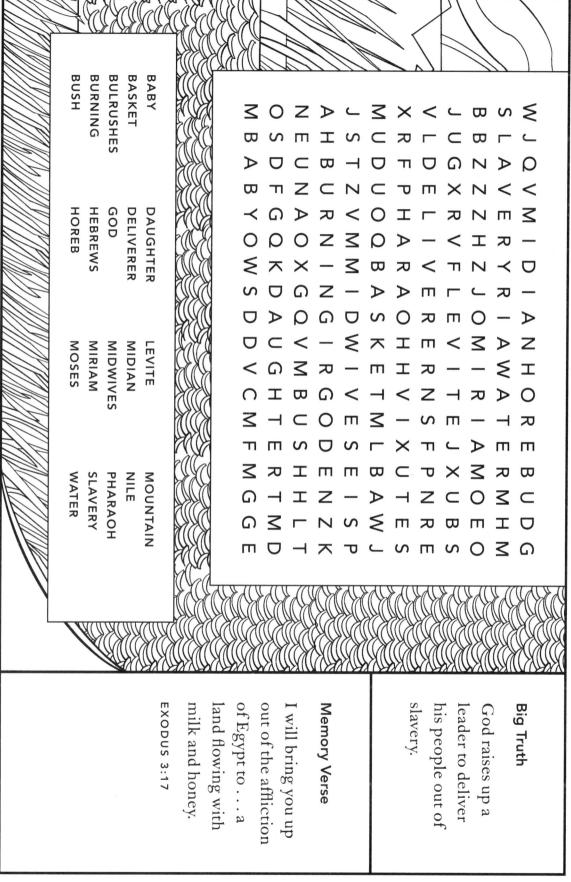

```
W J Q V M I D I A N H O R E B U D G
S L A V E R Y R I A W A T E R M H M
B B Z Z H Z J O M I R I A M O E O
J U G X R V F L E V I T E J X U B S
V L D E L I V E R E R N S F P N R E
X R F P H A R A O H H V I X U T E S
M U D U O Q B A S K E T M L B A W J
J S T Z V M M I D W I V E S E I S P
A H B U R N I N G I R G O D E N Z K
N E U N A O X G Q V M B U S H H L T
O S D F G Q K D A U G H T E R T M D
M B A B Y O W S D D V C M F M G G E
```

BABY	DAUGHTER	LEVITE	MOUNTAIN
BASKET	DELIVERER	MIDIAN	NILE
BULRUSHES	GOD	MIDWIVES	PHARAOH
BURNING	HEBREWS	MIRIAM	SLAVERY
BUSH	HOREB	MOSES	WATER

Big Truth

God raises up a leader to deliver his people out of slavery.

Memory Verse

I will bring you up out of the affliction of Egypt to . . . a land flowing with milk and honey.

EXODUS 3:17

Free at Last

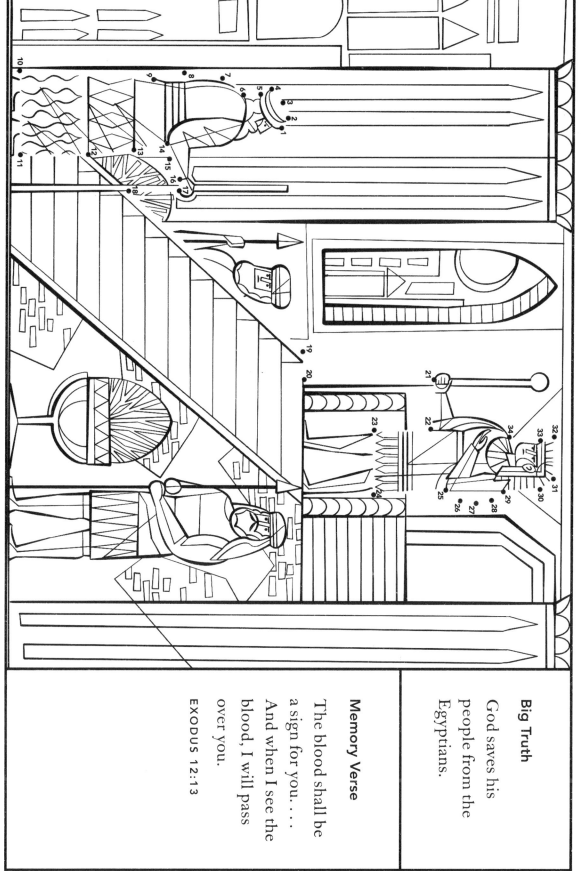

Big Truth

God saves his people from the Egyptians.

Memory Verse

The blood shall be a sign for you. . . . And when I see the blood, I will pass over you.

EXODUS 12:13

The Way to Stay Free

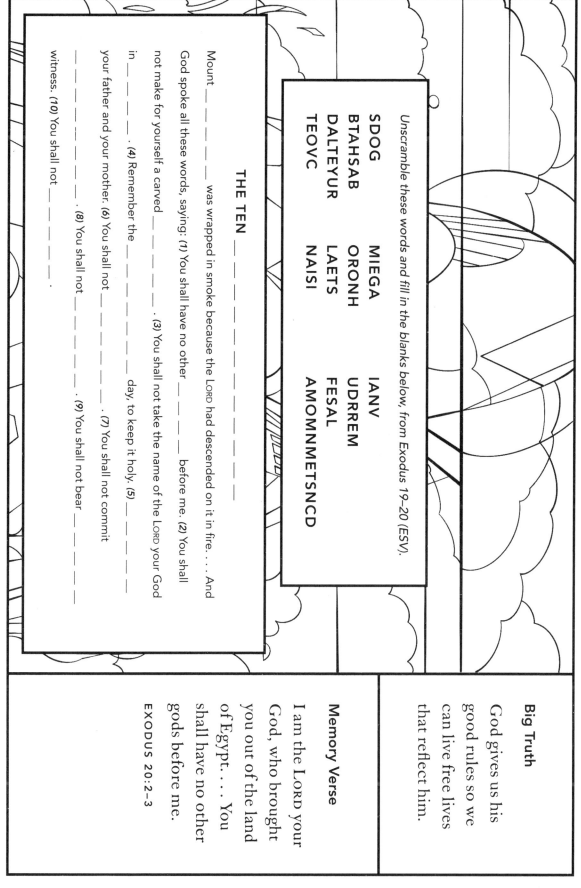

Unscramble these words and fill in the blanks below, from Exodus 19–20 (ESV).

SDOG	MIEGA	IANV	
BTAHSAB	ORONH	UDRREM	
DALTEYUR	LAETS	FESAL	
TEOVC	NAISI	AMOMNMMETSNCD	

THE TEN _____

Mount _____ was wrapped in smoke because the LORD had descended on it in fire. . . . And God spoke all these words, saying: **(1)** You shall have no other _____ before me. **(2)** You shall not make for yourself a carved _____ _____. **(3)** You shall not take the name of the LORD your God in _____. **(4)** Remember the _____ day, to keep it holy. **(5)** _____ your father and your mother. **(6)** You shall not _____. **(7)** You shall not commit _____. **(8)** You shall not _____. **(9)** You shall not bear _____ _____ witness. **(10)** You shall not _____ _____ _____.

Big Truth

God gives us his good rules so we can live free lives that reflect him.

Memory Verse

I am the LORD your God, who brought you out of the land of Egypt. . . . You shall have no other gods before me.

EXODUS 20:2–3

A Fancy Tent and a Foolish Cow

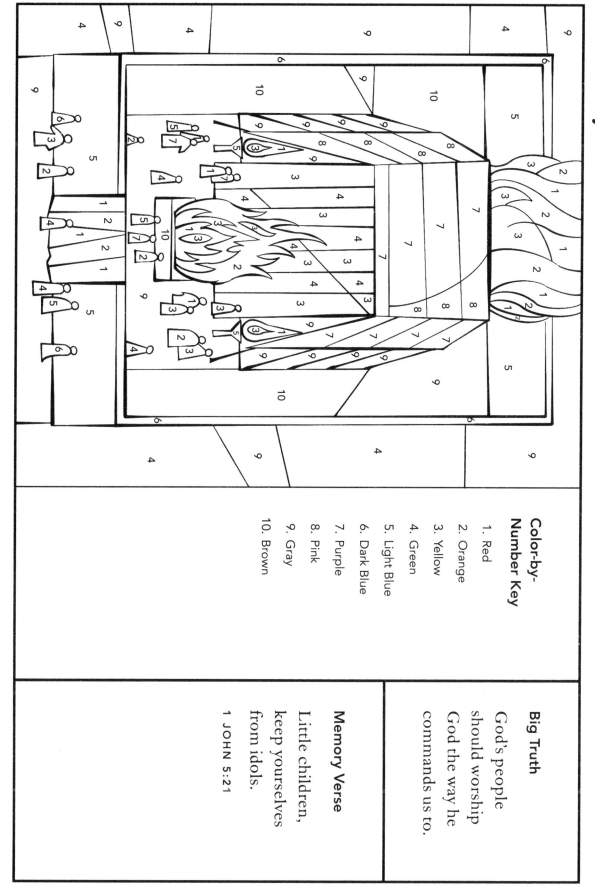

Color-by-Number Key

1. Red
2. Orange
3. Yellow
4. Green
5. Light Blue
6. Dark Blue
7. Purple
8. Pink
9. Gray
10. Brown

Big Truth

God's people should worship God the way he commands us to.

Memory Verse

Little children, keep yourselves from idols.

1 JOHN 5:21

A Tale of Two Goats

START

FINISH

Big Truth

God forgives and forgets our sins.

Memory Verse

We have been sanctified through the offering of the body of Jesus Christ once for all.

HEBREWS 10:10

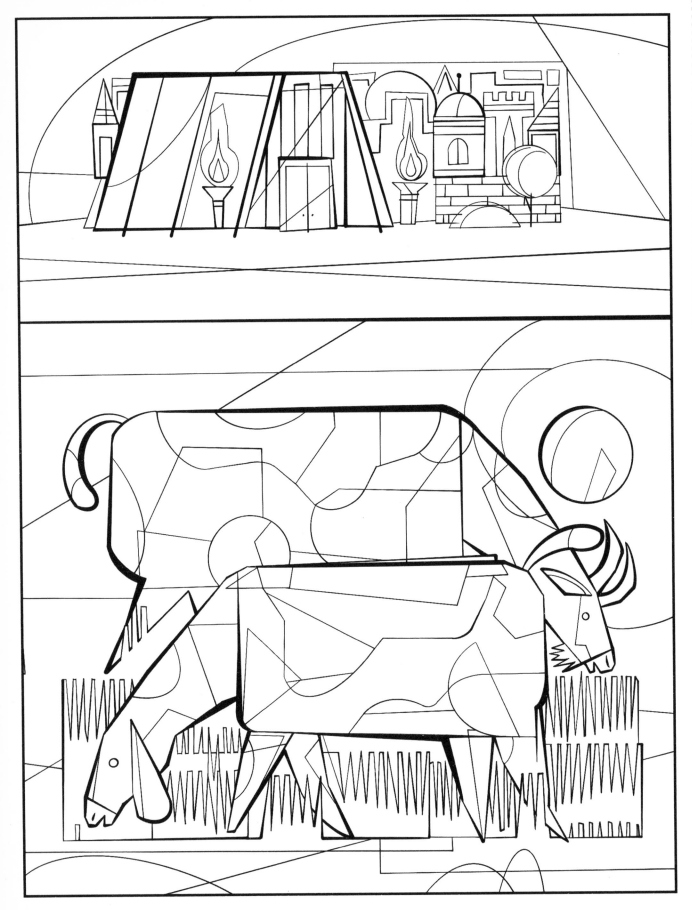

Story 17 • Leviticus 16 • A Tale of Two Goats

Big People, Little Faith

Find the items hidden in the picture.

FIVE GRAPE CLUSTERS

FIVE HONEY JARS

FIVE POMEGRANATES

FIVE FIGS

FIVE GIANTS

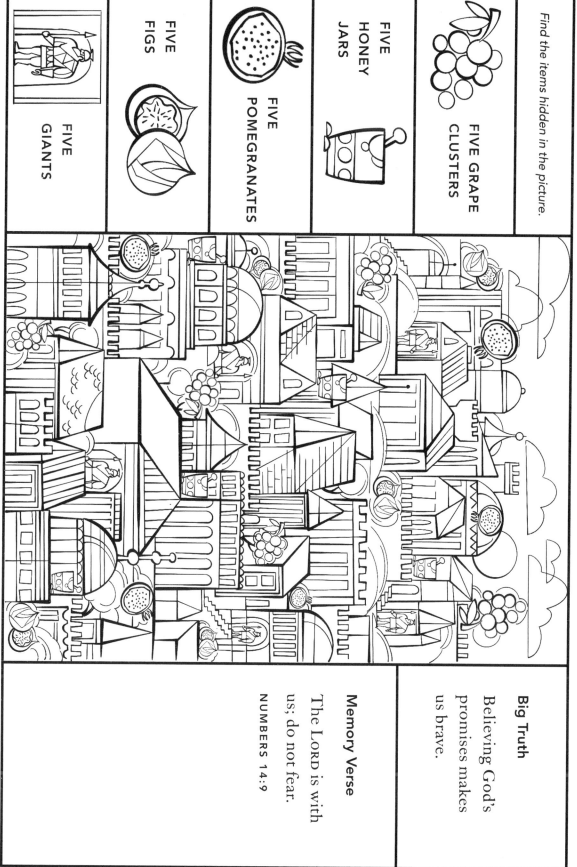

Big Truth

Believing God's promises makes us brave.

Memory Verse

The Lord is with us; do not fear.

NUMBERS 14:9

You're Not the Boss of Me

From Numbers 16 (ESV)

Across

2. A second leader of rebellion against Moses
5. This covered the tent of meeting
7. The place of worship for Israel
8. The son of Aaron
12. One of the leaders of rebellion
13. God sent a _____ against the people of Israel

Down

1. Aaron carried this to stop the plague
3. Korah claimed that the whole congregation was _____
4. The people _____ against Moses and Aaron
9. A third leader of rebellion against Moses
10. God's appointed leader of Israel
11. God's appointed high priest

6. It opened up to swallow them

Big Truth

God judges those who reject his plan and his chosen leaders.

Memory Verse

Know therefore today that he who goes over before you as a consuming fire is the LORD your God.

DEUTERONOMY 9:3

The Daughters of Zelophehad

```
P D I Q E H Y I H A M A F G C I S
O M B N Z O V V R R O L A V F O S N
S A K H T M I L C A H G T H Y M N Q
S N A E A T I R Z A H Z L R L M O Z
E A U R P R O M I S E S Z A H A A M
S S O I N E L O P H E H A D H N H O
I E I A L D Q N Z A T I N L H D X S
O H O N Z U R A K U X N I C V E T S
N Z L C O T R I B E S D B K A N U R
W C C E R P Z U L K P L F K E T Y D
Y E J W G D A U G H T E R S Y T K W
```

COMMANDMENT	MOSES
DAUGHTERS	NOAH
HOGLAH	POSSESSION
INHERITANCE	PROMISES
LAND	TIRZAH
MAHLAH	TRIBES
MANASSEH	ZELOPHEHAD
MILCAH	

Big Truth

God wants all his people to know all his blessing—nobody is left out.

Memory Verse

He [God] has caused us to be born again to a living hope through the resurrection of Jesus Christ from the dead, to an inheritance that is imperishable, undefiled, and unfading, kept in heaven for you.

1 PETER 1:3–4

The Walls Came Tumbling Down

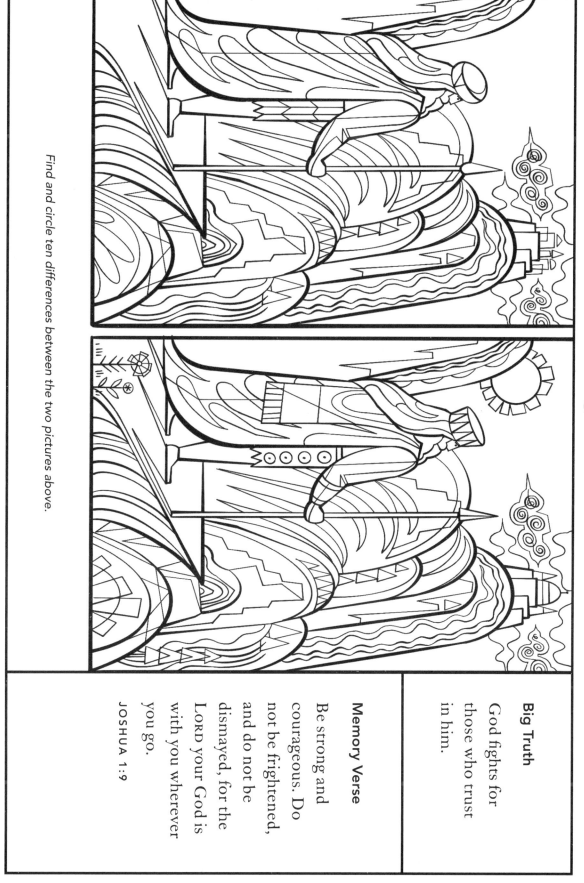

Find and circle ten differences between the two pictures above.

Big Truth

God fights for those who trust in him.

Memory Verse

Be strong and courageous. Do not be frightened, and do not be dismayed, for the LORD your God is with you wherever you go.

JOSHUA 1:9

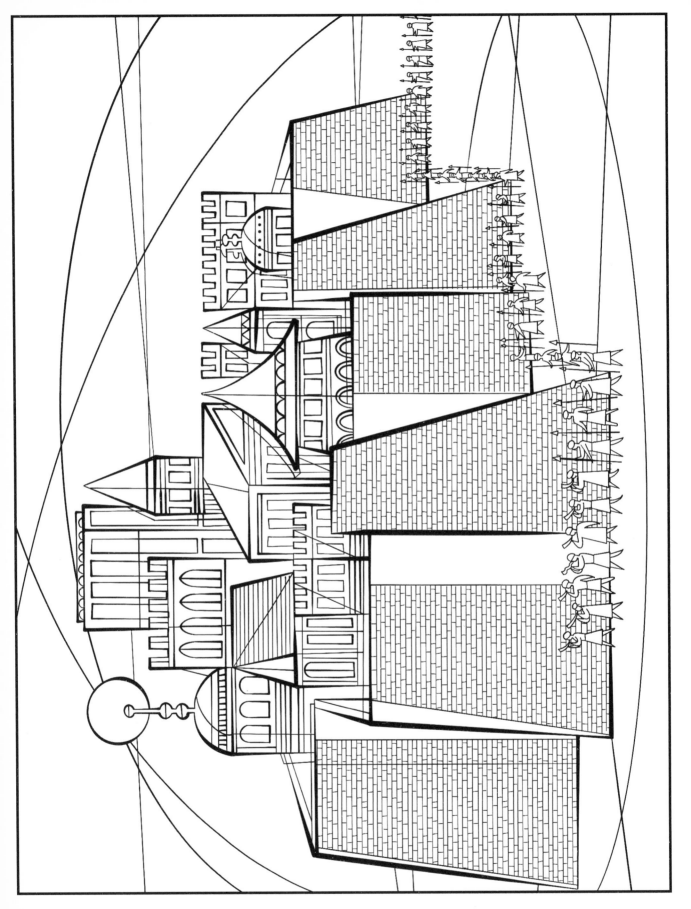

Story 21 • Joshua 6 • The Walls Came Tumbling Down

The Fight of Gideon and the Flight of Midian

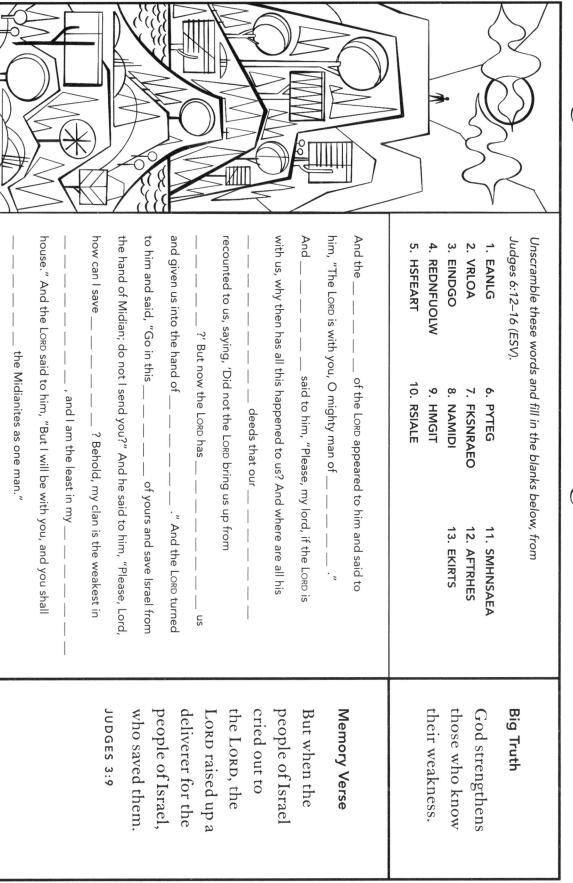

Unscramble these words and fill in the blanks below, from Judges 6:12-16 (ESV).

1. EANLG
2. VRLOA
3. EINDGO
4. REDNFUOLW
5. HSFEART

6. PYTEG
7. FKSNRAEO
8. NAMIDI
9. HMGIT
10. RSIALE

11. SMHNSAEA
12. AFTRHES
13. EKIRTS

And the ___ ___ of the LORD appeared to him and said to him, "The LORD is with you, O mighty man of ___ ___ ___ ___ ."

And ___ ___ said to him, "Please, my lord, if the LORD is with us, why then has all this happened to us? And where are all his ___ ___ ___ ___ deeds that our ___ ___ ___ ___ recounted to us, saying, 'Did not the LORD bring us up from ___ ___ ___ ___ ___ us ?' But now the LORD has ___ ___ ___ ___ ___ and given us into the hand of ___ ___ ___ ___ ." And the LORD turned to him and said, "Go in this ___ ___ ___ ___ of yours and save Israel from the hand of Midian; do not I send you?" And he said to him, "Please, Lord, how can I save ___ ___ ___ ___ ? Behold, my clan is the weakest in ___ ___ ___ ___ ___ , and I am the least in my ___ ___ ___ ___ house." And the LORD said to him, "But I will be with you, and you shall ___ ___ ___ ___ the Midianites as one man."

Big Truth

God strengthens those who know their weakness.

Memory Verse

But when the people of Israel cried out to the LORD, the LORD raised up a deliverer for the people of Israel, who saved them.

JUDGES 3:9

Story 22 • Judges 6–7 • The Fight of Gideon and the Flight of Midian

Samson's Strength

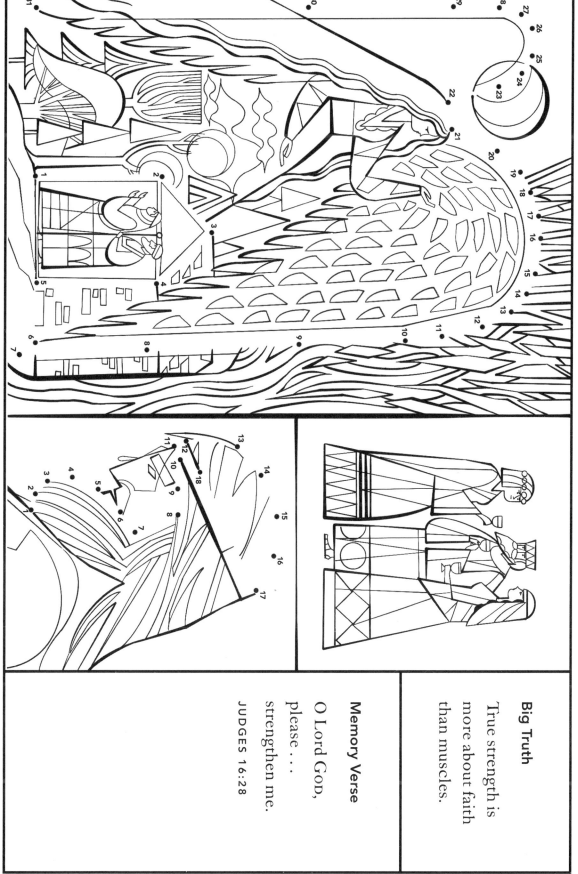

Big Truth

True strength is more about faith than muscles.

Memory Verse

O Lord GOD, please . . . strengthen me.

JUDGES 16:28

The Girl Who Wouldn't Go Away

Color-by-Number Key

1. Red
2. Orange
3. Light Green
4. Dark Green
5. Light Blue
6. Dark Blue
7. Purple
8. Pink
9. Gray
10. Black

Big Truth

We can trust God's plan for our lives even when things don't go our way.

Memory Verse

Blessed be the LORD, who has not left you this day without a redeemer!

RUTH 4:14

Story 24 • Ruth 1–4 • The Girl Who Wouldn't Go Away

The Lord's Word and Samuel

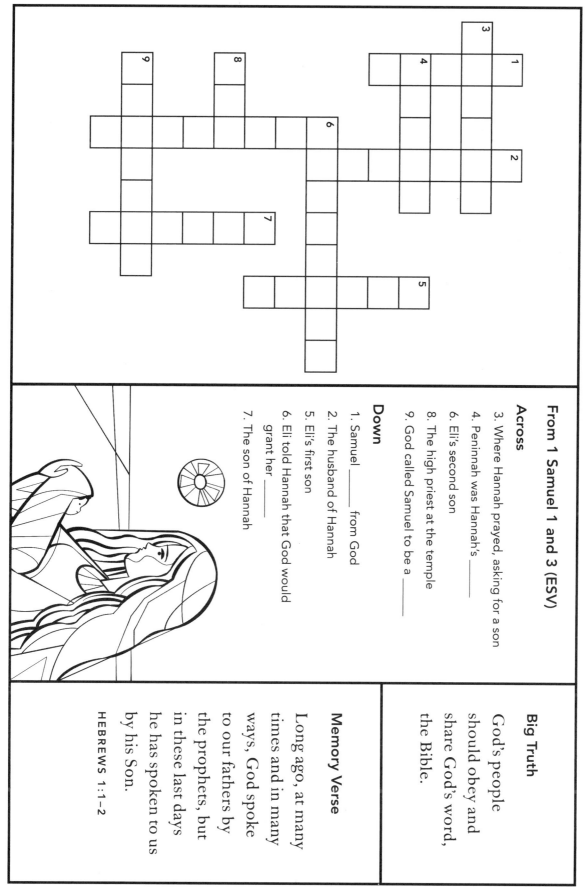

From 1 Samuel 1 and 3 (ESV)

Across

3. Where Hannah prayed, asking for a son
4. Peninnah was Hannah's ____
6. Eli's second son
8. The high priest at the temple
9. God called Samuel to be a ____

Down

1. Samuel ____ from God
2. The husband of Hannah
5. Eli's first son
6. Eli told Hannah that God would grant her ____
7. The son of Hannah

Big Truth

God's people should obey and share God's word, the Bible.

Memory Verse

Long ago, at many times and in many ways, God spoke to our fathers by the prophets, but in these last days he has spoken to us by his Son.

HEBREWS 1:1–2

Story 25 • 1 Samuel 1; 3 • The Lord's Word and Samuel

The Rise and Fall of King Saul

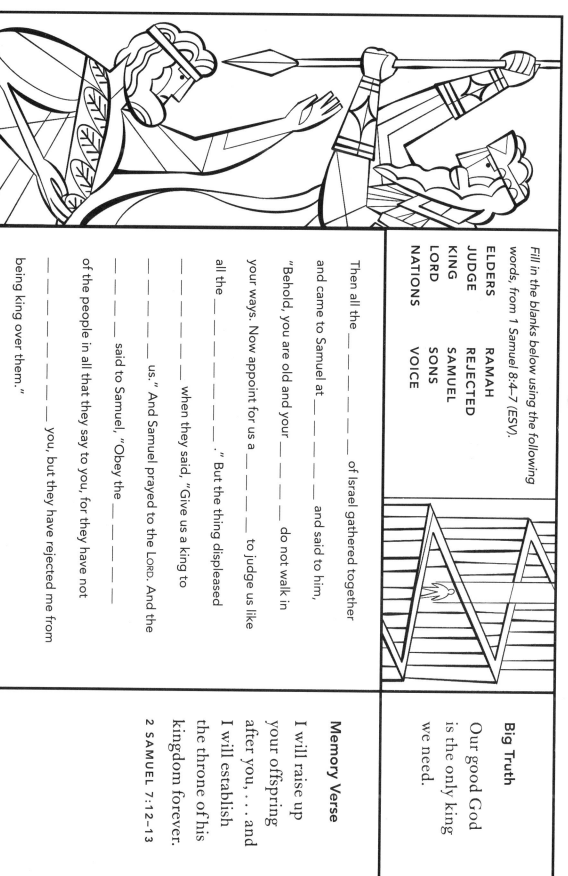

Fill in the blanks below using the following words, from 1 Samuel 8:4–7 (ESV).

ELDERS	RAMAH
JUDGE	REJECTED
KING	SAMUEL
LORD	SONS
NATIONS	VOICE

Then all the — — — — — — of Israel gathered together and came to Samuel at — — — — — and said to him, "Behold, you are old and your — — — — do not walk in your ways. Now appoint for us a — — — — to judge us like all the — — — — — — — ." But the thing displeased — — — — — — when they said, "Give us a king to — — — — — us." And Samuel prayed to the LORD. And the — — — — said to Samuel, "Obey the — — — — — of the people in all that they say to you, for they have not — — — — — — — you, but they have rejected me from being king over them."

Big Truth

Our good God is the only king we need.

Memory Verse

I will raise up your offspring after you, . . . and I will establish the throne of his kingdom forever.

2 SAMUEL 7:12–13

Story 26 • 1 Samuel 8–15 • The Rise and Fall of King Saul

David Stands Tall

Find the items hidden in the picture below.

SLING

CROWN

LYRE

HORN OF OIL

FIVE SMOOTH STONES

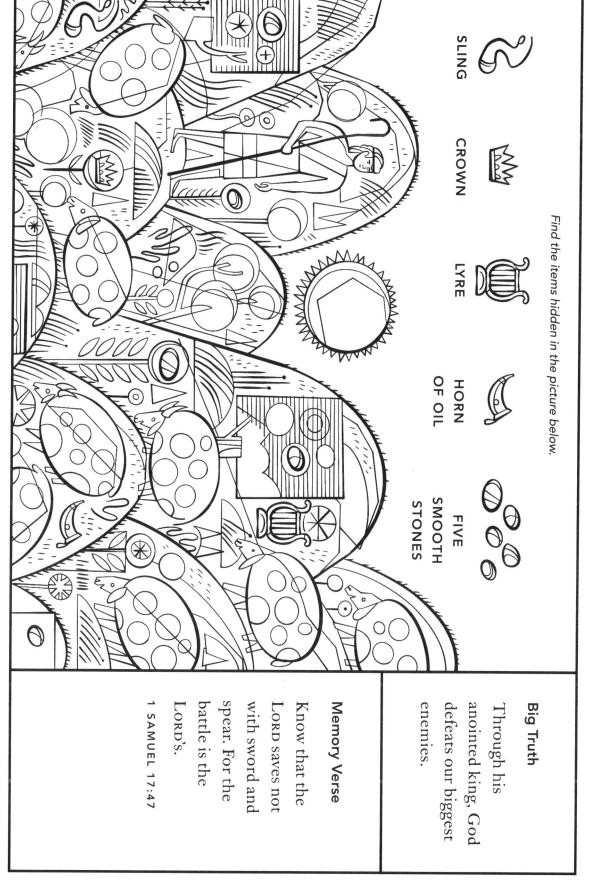

Big Truth

Through his anointed king, God defeats our biggest enemies.

Memory Verse

Know that the LORD saves not with sword and spear. For the battle is the LORD's.

1 SAMUEL 17:47

David Stands Tall • 1 Samuel 16–17 • Story 27

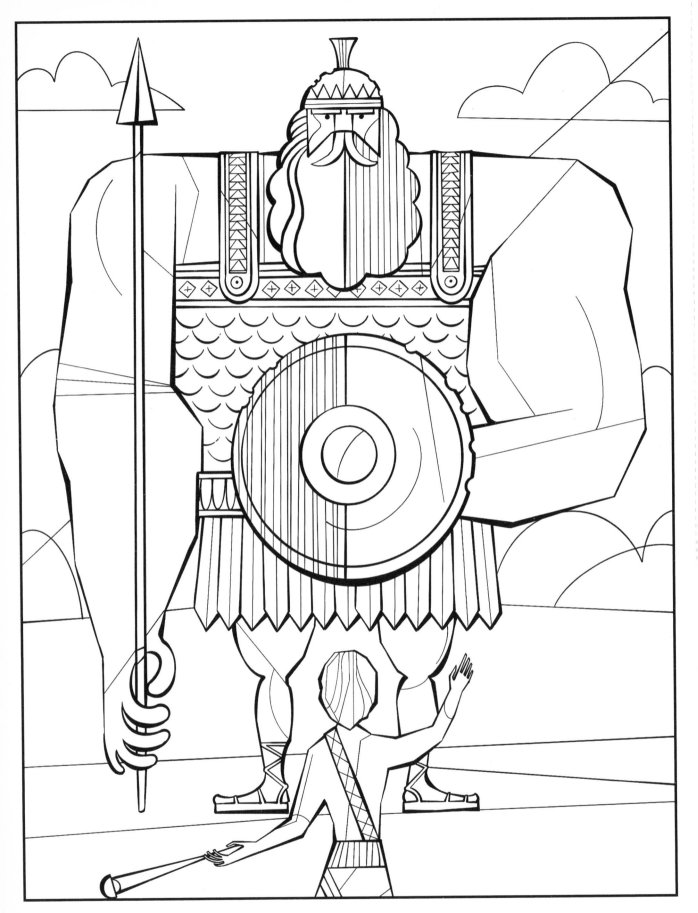

David Sins . . . and Repents

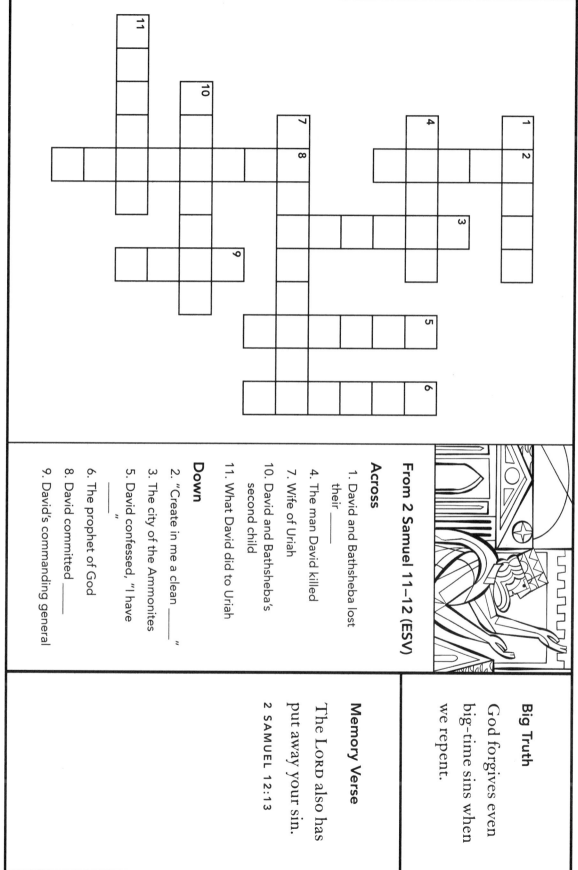

From 2 Samuel 11–12 (ESV)

Across

1. David and Bathsheba lost their _____
4. The man David killed
7. Wife of Uriah
10. David and Bathsheba's second child
11. What David did to Uriah

Down

2. "Create in me a clean _____ "
3. The city of the Ammonites
5. David confessed, "I have _____ "
6. The prophet of God
8. David committed _____
9. David's commanding general

Big Truth

God forgives even big-time sins when we repent.

Memory Verse

The LORD also has put away your sin.

2 SAMUEL 12:13

Story 28 • 2 Samuel 11–12 • David Sins . . . and Repents

The Wise and Foolish King

Unscramble the words below, from the story of King Solomon in 1 Kings 3 and 11 (ESV).

MNSOOLO _____

DOISWM _____

EYARPR _____

TEUSJIC _____

WIVSE _____

YEPTG _____

BOMA _____

OEDM _____

SGDO _____

VIEL _____

GMDNOKI _____

Big Truth

God can give us wisdom to live for him.

Memory Verse

If any of you lacks wisdom, let him ask God, who gives generously to all without reproach, and it will be given him.

JAMES 1:5

The Wise and Foolish King • 1 Kings 3; 11 • Story 29

Story 29 • 1 Kings 3; 11 • The Wise and Foolish King

The Kingdom Cracks

```
S H U M P K T R W W I G L T A Y N C
S P L I T E S H T P X F Q R J M E
Z W C C J S C J R W X T C I N U P B
J R O N Y C C A U O O K Y B I Q Q L
E Y U C U O C Q L D N P F E I D O S
R B N I A R U G X V A E B S K G S I
O B S S C P D B O X E H W I P S H
B B E R W I S K K L P S P R E A W E
O H L A F O X M U L D A U Q T B K A
A B Z E C N J J V D E Y U E I B V
M I K L L S Y O K E Q B N U N Q K Y
W R E H O B O A M I K B H L U J Z M
```

CALVES	SCORPIONS
COUNSEL	SPLIT
GOLDEN	TEN
HEAVY	THRONE
ISRAEL	TRIBES
JEROBOAM	TWO
JUDAH	WHIPS
REHOBOAM	YOKE

Big Truth

Two bad kings cracked God's kingdom.

Memory Verse

Pride goes before destruction, and a haughty spirit before a fall.

PROVERBS 16:18

Elijah Proves a Point

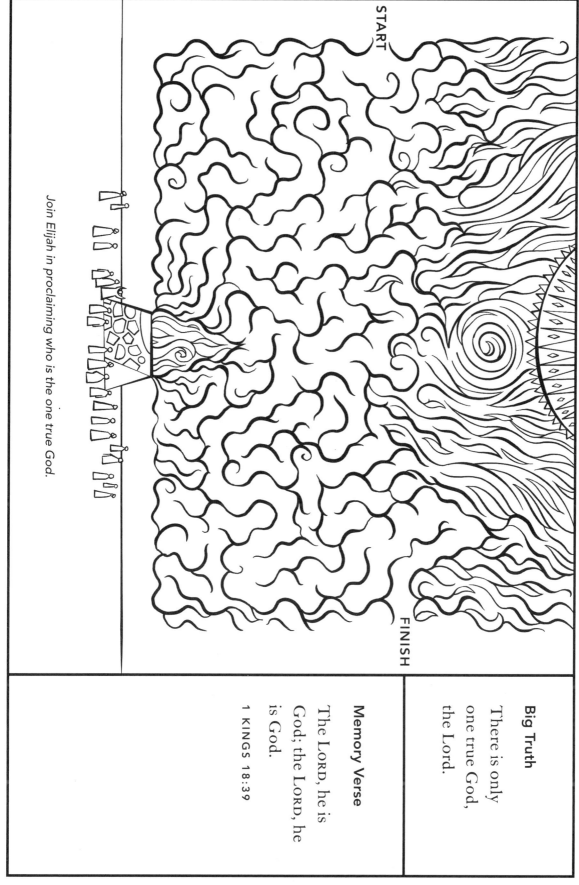

START

FINISH

Join Elijah in proclaiming who is the one true God.

Big Truth

There is only one true God, the Lord.

Memory Verse

The LORD, he is God; the LORD, he is God.

1 KINGS 18:39

Grime and Punishment

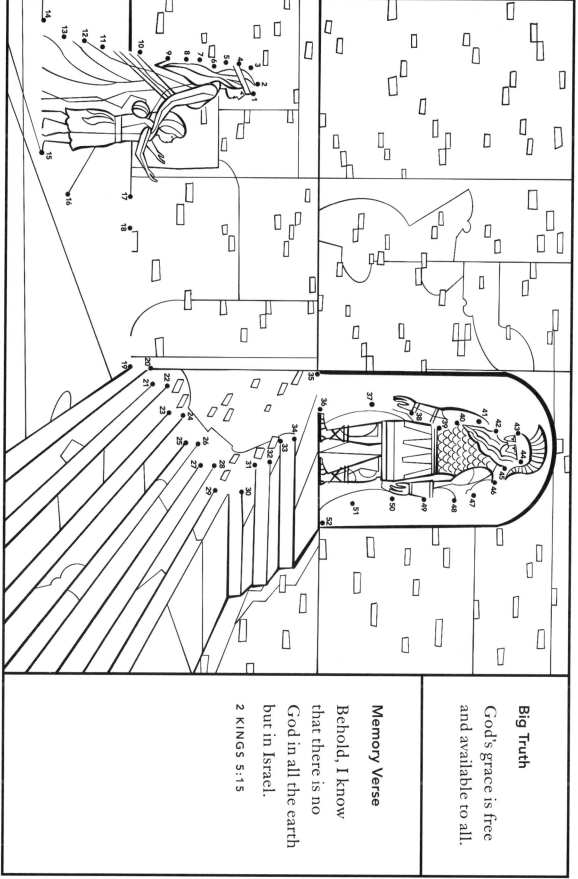

Big Truth

God's grace is free and available to all.

Memory Verse

Behold, I know that there is no God in all the earth but in Israel.

2 KINGS 5:15

The Boy Who Sought the Lord

Help Josiah locate the law of God.

START

FINISH

Big Truth

God's people must worship the right God in the right way.

Memory Verse

If my people who are called by my name humble themselves, and pray and seek my face and turn from their wicked ways, then I will hear from heaven and will forgive their sin and heal their land.

2 CHRONICLES 7:14

Promises Broken and Promises Kept

Fill in the blanks below using the following words, from 2 Chronicles 36:15–17 (ESV):

LORD	MESSENGERS	COMPASSION	MOCKING
WRATH	DESPISING	PROPHETS	REMEDY
SWORD	AGAINST	COMPASSION	HAND

The ———, the God of their fathers, sent persistently to them by his ———————, because he had —— —— on his people and on his dwelling place. But they kept scoffing at his ———————, ————— his words and ——— the messengers of God, ————— his ———, until the ——— of the LORD rose against his people, until there was no ———. Therefore he brought up —— —— —— —— them the king of the Chaldeans, who killed their young men with the ——— in the house of their sanctuary and had no ——— on young man or virgin, old man or aged. He gave them all into his ——— ———.

Big Truth

God cursed his people for breaking their promise.

Memory Verse

They kept mocking the messengers of God, despising his words and scoffing at his prophets, until the wrath of the LORD rose against his people.

2 CHRONICLES 36:16

Walls and Worship

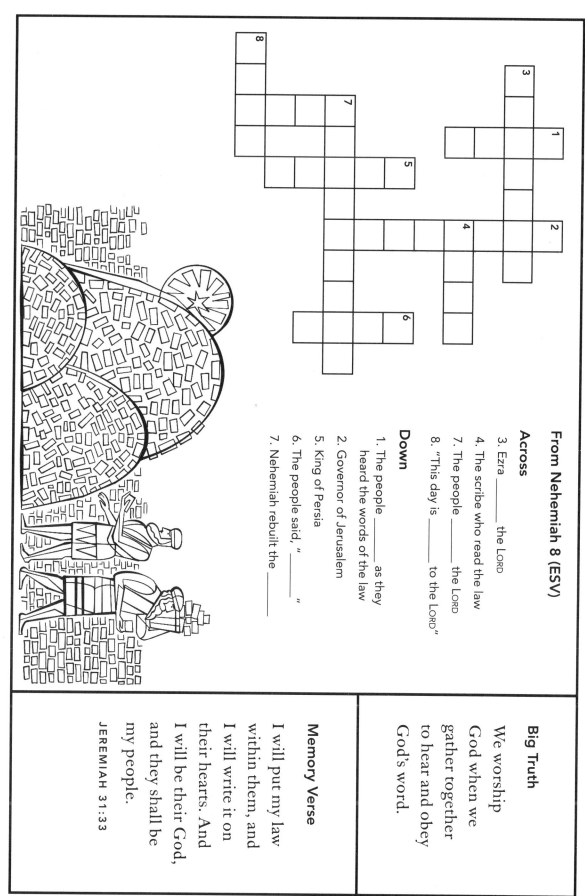

From Nehemiah 8 (ESV)

Across

3. Ezra _____ the LORD
4. The scribe who read the law
7. The people _____ the LORD
8. "This day is _____ to the LORD "

Down

1. The people _____ as they heard the words of the law
2. Governor of Jerusalem
5. King of Persia
6. The people said, " _____ "
7. Nehemiah rebuilt the _____

Big Truth

We worship God when we gather together to hear and obey God's word.

Memory Verse

I will put my law within them, and I will write it on their hearts. And I will be their God, and they shall be my people.

JEREMIAH 31:33

More Than a Pretty Face

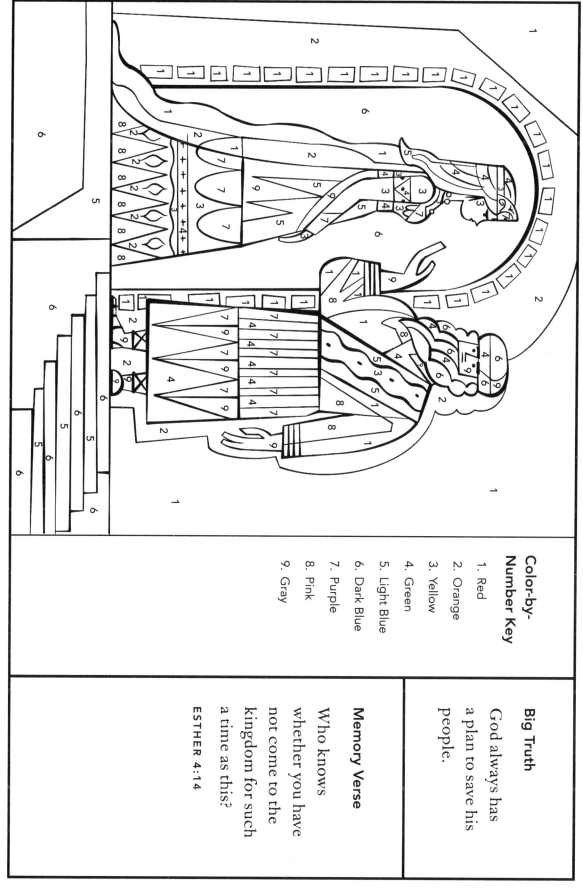

Color-by-Number Key

1. Red
2. Orange
3. Yellow
4. Green
5. Light Blue
6. Dark Blue
7. Purple
8. Pink
9. Gray

Big Truth

God always has a plan to save his people.

Memory Verse

Who knows whether you have not come to the kingdom for such a time as this?

ESTHER 4:14

A Hard Life and a Good God

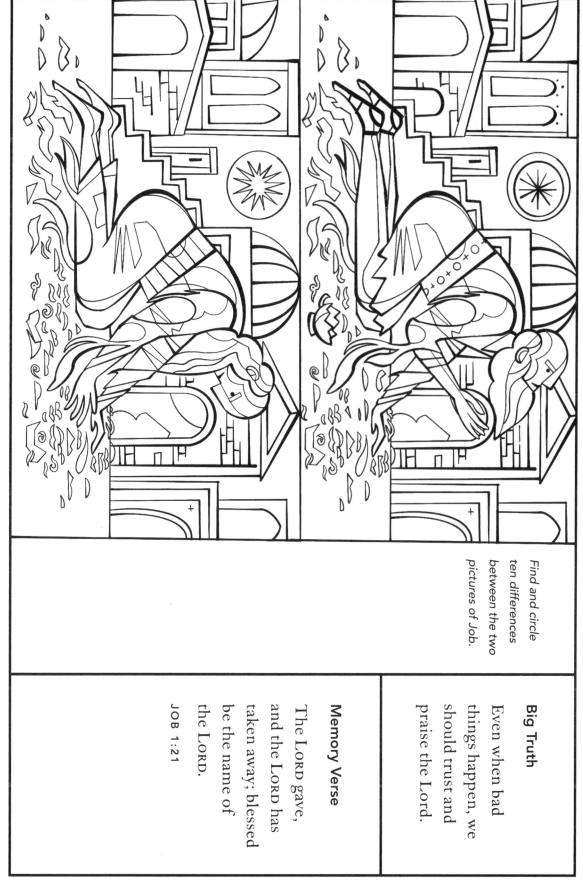

Find and circle
ten differences
between the two
pictures of Job.

Big Truth

Even when bad
things happen, we
should trust and
praise the Lord.

Memory Verse

The LORD gave,
and the LORD has
taken away; blessed
be the name of
the LORD.

JOB 1:21

Story 37 • Job 1 • A Hard Life and a Good God

Cover Your Mouth

From Job 38–42 (ESV)

Across

2. "Can you bind the chains of the ____?"

3. "Have you comprehended the ____?"

6. "Where were you when I laid the ____ of the earth?"

7. "Who is it that darkens counsel by words without ____?"

9. "Who has begotten the drops of ____?"

10. "Where is the way to the dwelling of ____?"

Down

1. "Do you know the ____ of the heavens?"

4. "Have you seen the gates of deep ____?"

5. "Have you commanded the ____ since your days began?"

8. "Who can number the clouds by ____?"

Big Truth

God is God, and we are not! We should trust him when things are hard.

Memory Verse

I know that you can do all things, and that no purpose of yours can be thwarted.

JOB 42:2

The Lord Is My Shepherd

START

FINISH

Big Truth

God, as our shepherd, leads, feeds, protects, and forgives us.

Memory Verse

The LORD is my shepherd; I shall not want.

PSALM 23:1

The Beginning of Wisdom

Unscramble the words below, from Proverbs 1 (ESV).

WSMDOI _____

OTRNNCISUIT _____

OEHNUSSERSTGI _____

CTUIJES _____

PUNCEDER _____

IEQYUT _____

VPEBROR _____

ARFE _____

OFLOS _____

EFRATH _____

MHTOER _____

EPISML _____

Big Truth

Fearing God makes us wise.

Memory Verse

The fear of the Lord is the beginning of knowledge.

PROVERBS 1:7

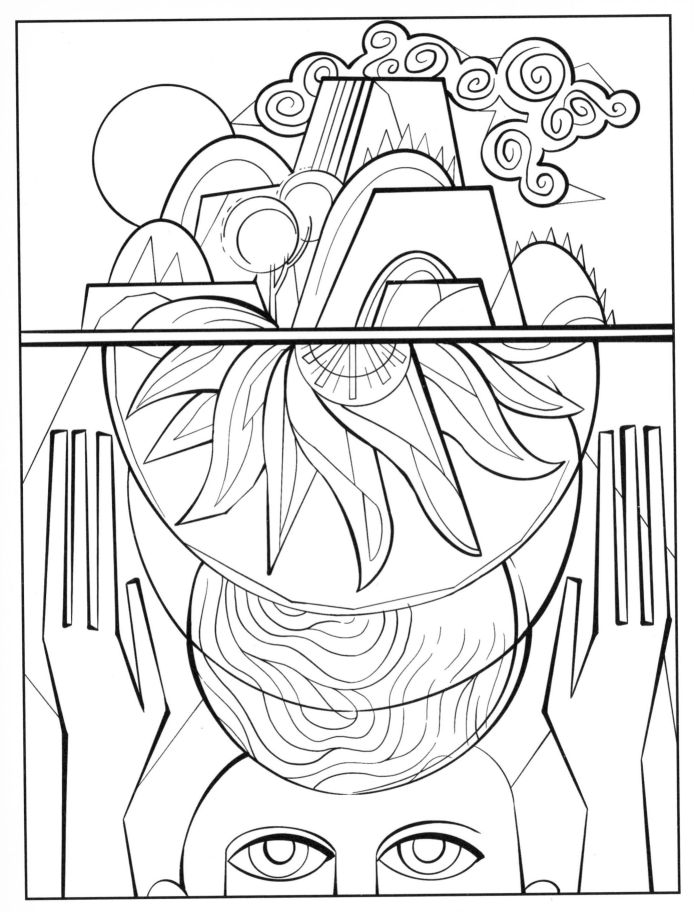

What Isaiah Saw

Color-by-Number Key

1. Red
2. Orange
3. Yellow
4. Green
5. Light Blue
6. Dark Blue
7. Purple
8. Pink
9. Black

Big Truth

God is holy, and only God can make us holy.

Memory Verse

Holy, holy, holy is the Lord of hosts; the whole earth is full of his glory!

ISAIAH 6:3

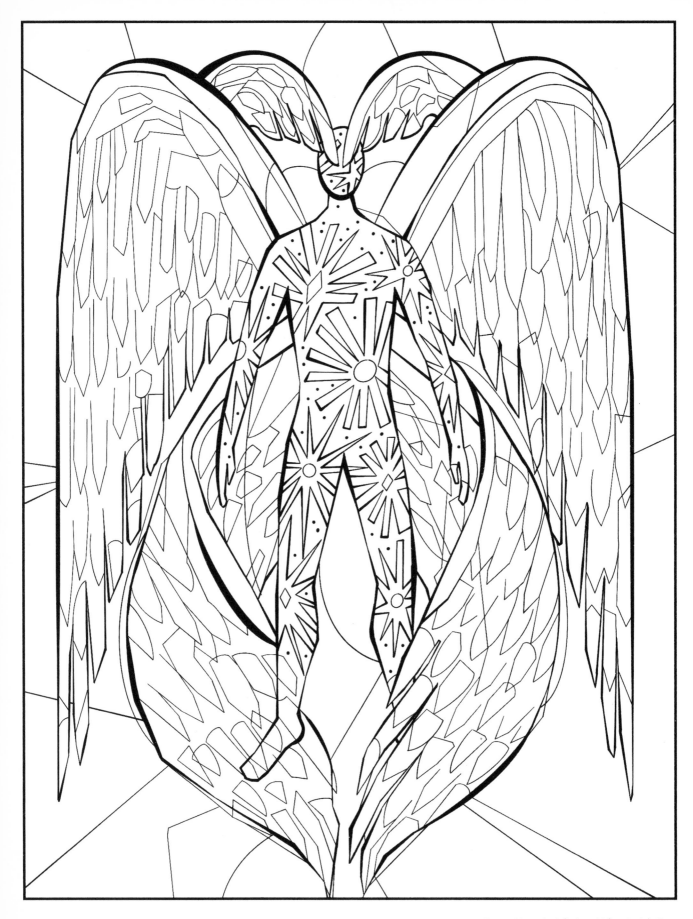

Jeremiah against Everyone

Unscramble the words below, from Jeremiah 1 (ESV).

WROD _____

WBOM _____

TOAECSDNREC _____

OHPTPRE _____

EPSAK _____

UYTOH _____

MONCDMA _____

EDLERIV _____

SRODW _____

DMKOSING _____

LPCUK _____

KREAB _____

DIULB _____

TLAPN _____

Big Truth

When we stand with God, he is for us even when everyone is against us.

Memory Verse

Do not be afraid of them, for I am with you to deliver you, declares the LORD.

JEREMIAH 1:8

The Valley of Dry Bones

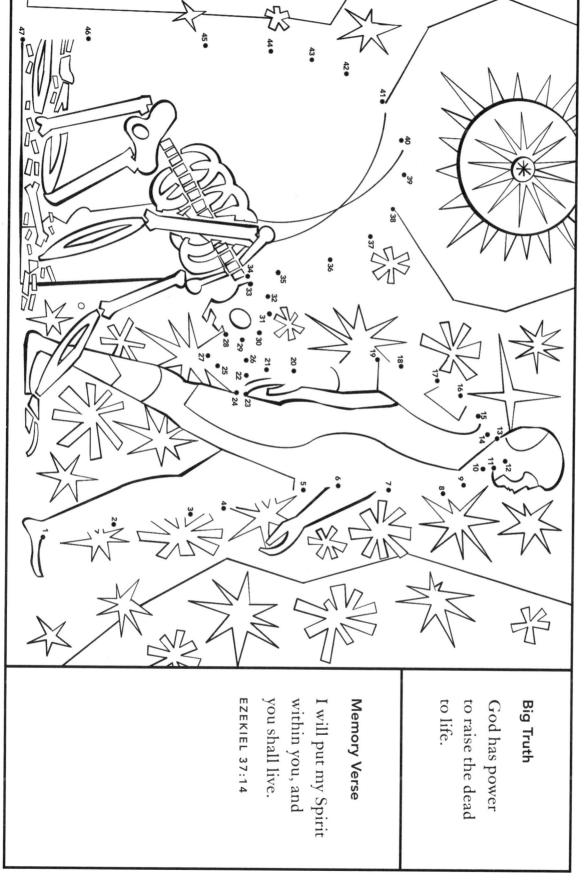

Big Truth

God has power
to raise the dead
to life.

Memory Verse

I will put my Spirit
within you, and
you shall live.

EZEKIEL 37:14

The Fiery Furnace

Unscramble the words below, from the story of the fiery furnace in Daniel 3 (ESV).

NCNHDAZZERAUEB _____

ABYBNLO _____

EGMAI _____

IOWPHRS _____

CAFEURN _____

ASDCHAHR _____

MACEHSH _____

ANGDBOEE _____

NLGEOD _____

EEVEDLRRI _____

RUFO _____

Big Truth

God's people should put God first no matter what.

Memory Verse

You shall not make for yourself a carved image, or any likeness of anything that is in heaven above, or that is in the earth beneath, or that is in the water under the earth.

EXODUS 20:4

Writing on the Wall

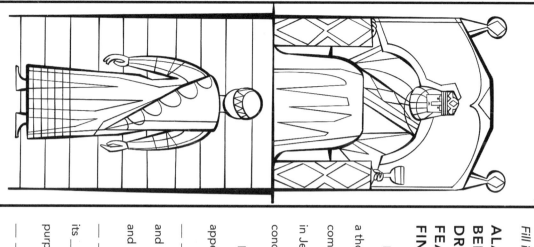

Fill in the blanks below using these words, from Daniel 5 (ESV):

ALARMED	GOLD	RULER
BELSHAZZAR	HAND	TEMPLE
DRINK	INTERPRETATION	WISE
FEAST	KING	WROTE
FINGERS	KNEES	

King — — — — — — — — — — made a great — — — — — — for

a thousand of his lords and drank wine in front of the thousand. Belshazzar

commanded that the vessels that had been taken out of the — — — — — —

in Jerusalem be brought, that the king and his lords, his wives, and his

concubines might — — — — — — from them.

Immediately the — — — — — — — — of a human — — — —

appeared and — — — — — — — on the wall of the king's palace. And the

— — — — saw the hand as it wrote. Then the king's color changed,

and his thoughts — — — — — — — — him; his limbs gave way,

and his — — — — — — knocked together. The king declared to the

— — — — — men of Babylon, "Whoever reads this writing, and shows me

its — — — — — — — — — — — , shall be clothed with

purple and have a chain of — — — — — around his neck and shall be the third

— — — — — — in the kingdom."

Big Truth

God is so powerful
that he controls
kings and
kingdoms.

Memory Verse

God opposes
the proud but
gives grace to the
humble.

JAMES 4:6

The Miraculous Catnap

Help Daniel out of the lions' den.

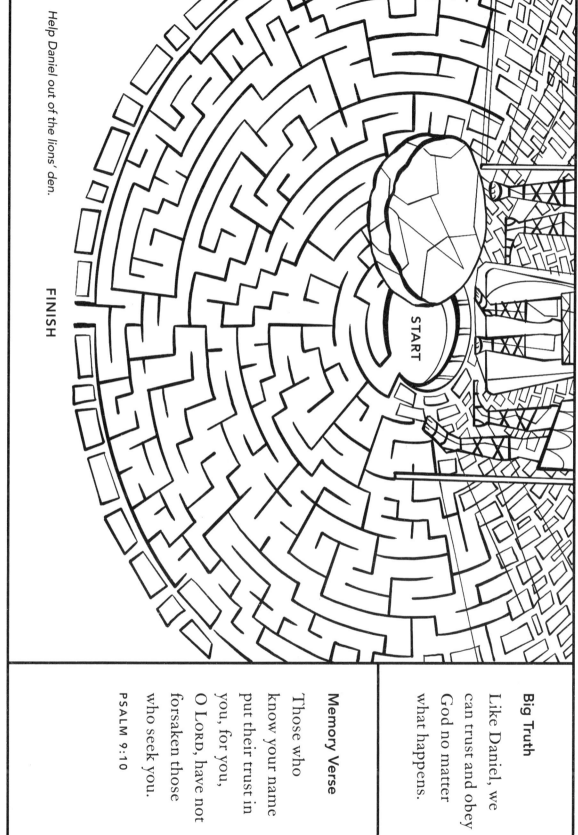

START

FINISH

Big Truth

Like Daniel, we can trust and obey God no matter what happens.

Memory Verse

Those who know your name put their trust in you, for you, O LORD, have not forsaken those who seek you.

PSALM 9:10

A Marriage Made in Heaven

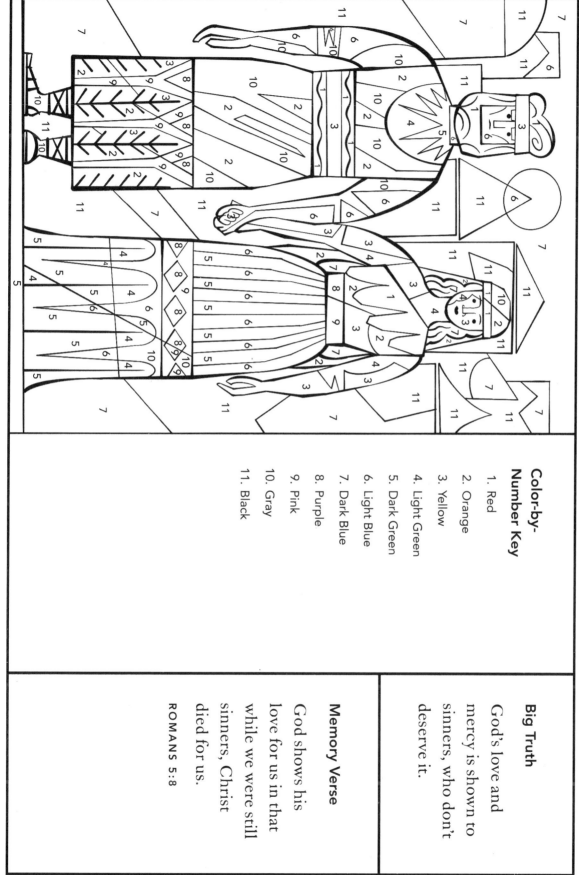

Color-by-Number Key

1. Red
2. Orange
3. Yellow
4. Light Green
5. Dark Green
6. Light Blue
7. Dark Blue
8. Purple
9. Pink
10. Gray
11. Black

Big Truth

God's love and mercy is shown to sinners, who don't deserve it.

Memory Verse

God shows his love for us in that while we were still sinners, Christ died for us.

ROMANS 5:8

Story 47 • Hosea 1–3 • A Marriage Made in Heaven

Let Justice Roll Down

From Amos 5 (ESV)

(4)_____ the LORD and live, lest he break out like fire in the house of Joseph, and it devour, with none to quench it for Bethel, O you who turn justice to (1)_____ and cast down righteousness to the earth! . . . Seek (9)_____, and not (8)_____, that you may live; and so the LORD, the God of hosts, will be with you, as you have said. Hate evil, and love good, and establish (10)_____ in the gate; it may be that the LORD, the God of hosts, will be (6)_____ to the remnant of Joseph. . . . But let justice roll down like (2)_____, and (5)_____ like an ever-(3)_____ (7)_____.

Big Truth

God wants his people to hate evil, love good, and seek justice.

Memory Verse

Let justice roll down like waters.

AMOS 5:24

Famine and Feast

START

FINISH

Big Truth

God's people should worship the God who speaks and saves by loving him and loving others.

Memory Verse

Man does not live by bread alone, but man lives by every word that comes from the mouth of the LORD.

DEUTERONOMY 8:3

Big Fish, Bigger Mercy

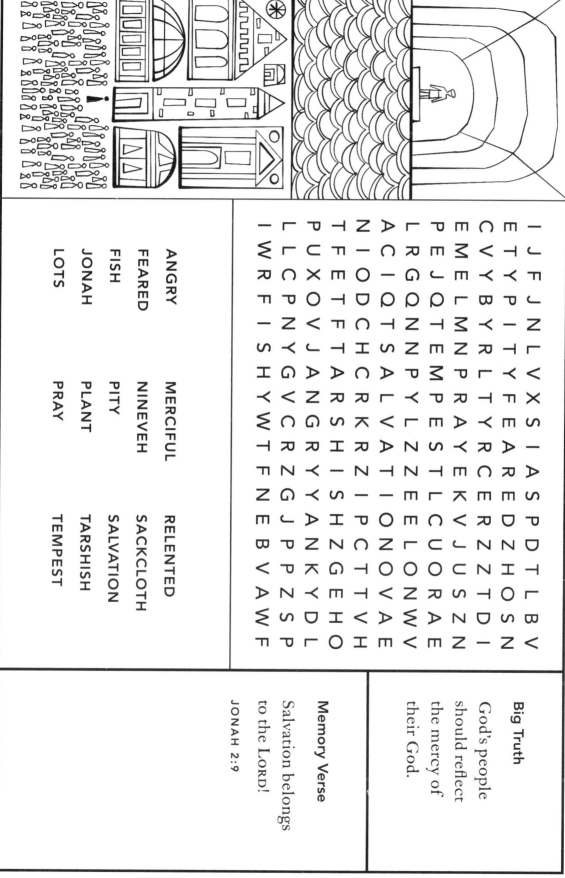

I J F J N L V X S I A S P D T L B V
E T Y P I T Y F E A R E D Z H O S N
C V Y B Y R L T Y R C E R Z N T D I
E M E L M N P R A Y E K V J U S Z N
P E J Q T E M P E S T L C U O R A E
L R G Q N N P Y L Z N E E L O N W V
A C I Q T S A L V A T I O N O V A E
N I O D C H C R K R N I P C T T V H
T F E T T A R S H I S H Z G E H O H
P U X O V J A N G R Y Y A N K Y D L
L L C P N Y G V C R Z N G J P P Z S P
I W R F I S H Y W T F N E B V A W F

ANGRY	MERCIFUL	RELENTED	
FEARED	NINEVEH	SACKCLOTH	
FISH	PITY	SALVATION	
JONAH	PLANT	TARSHISH	
LOTS	PRAY	TEMPEST	

Big Truth

God's people should reflect the mercy of their God.

Memory Verse

Salvation belongs to the LORD!

JONAH 2:9

A Change of Clothes

Fill in the blanks below using the following words, from Zechariah 3:6–10 (ESV):

ACCESS	**DECLARES**	**SIGN**
ANGEL	**INIQUITY**	**STONE**
BEHOLD	**INSCRIPTION**	**VINE**
BRANCH	**LORD**	**WAYS**
COURTS	**PRIEST**	

And the — — — — — of the — — — — — solemnly assured Joshua, "Thus says the LORD of hosts: If you will walk in my — — — — — and keep my charge, then you shall rule my house and have charge of my — — — — — , and I will give you the right of — — — — — among those who are standing here. Hear now, O Joshua the high — — — — — , you and your friends who sit before you, for they are men who are a — — — — — : behold, I will bring my servant the — — — — — . For — — — — — , on the stone that I have set before Joshua, on a single — — — — — with seven eyes, I will engrave its — — — — — , declares the LORD of hosts, and I will remove the — — — — — of this land in a single day. In that day, — — — — — the LORD of hosts, every one of you will invite his neighbor to come under his — — — — — and under his fig tree."

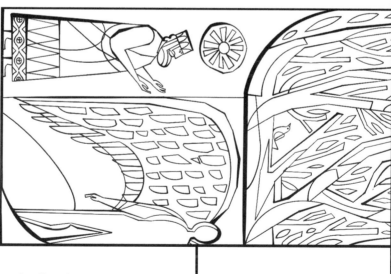

Big Truth

We are terribly dirty, but God makes us perfectly clean!

Memory Verse

Behold, I have taken your iniquity away from you, and I will clothe you with pure vestments.

ZECHARIAH 3:4

The Great and Awesome Day of the Lord

Malachi 3:1–3 (ESV)

Behold, I send my (1)_____, and he will (10)_____ the way before me. And the Lord whom you seek will suddenly come to his temple; and the messenger of the (2)_____ in whom you delight, behold, he is coming, says the LORD of hosts. But who can (4)_____ the day of his coming, and who can stand when he appears? For he is like a refiner's (11)_____ and like fullers' (8)_____. He will sit as a (3)_____ and (5)_____ of silver, and he will purify the sons of Levi and refine them like (9)_____ and (7)_____, and they will bring offerings in (6)_____ to the LORD.

Big Truth

Because of our Savior, all who turn to God have a great future!

Memory Verse

For you who fear my name, the sun of righteousness shall rise with healing in its wings.

MALACHI 4:2

Story 52 • Malachi 3–4 • The Great and Awesome Day of the Lord

A New Baby and a New Beginning

FINISH

START

Help Mary and Joseph find their way to the stable in Bethlehem.

Big Truth

Jesus was born to save his people from their sin.

Memory Verse

She [Mary] will bear a son, and you [Joseph] shall call his name Jesus, for he will save his people from their sins.

MATTHEW 1:21

Story 53 • Matthew 1 • A New Baby and a New Beginning

Wise Men, Smart Move

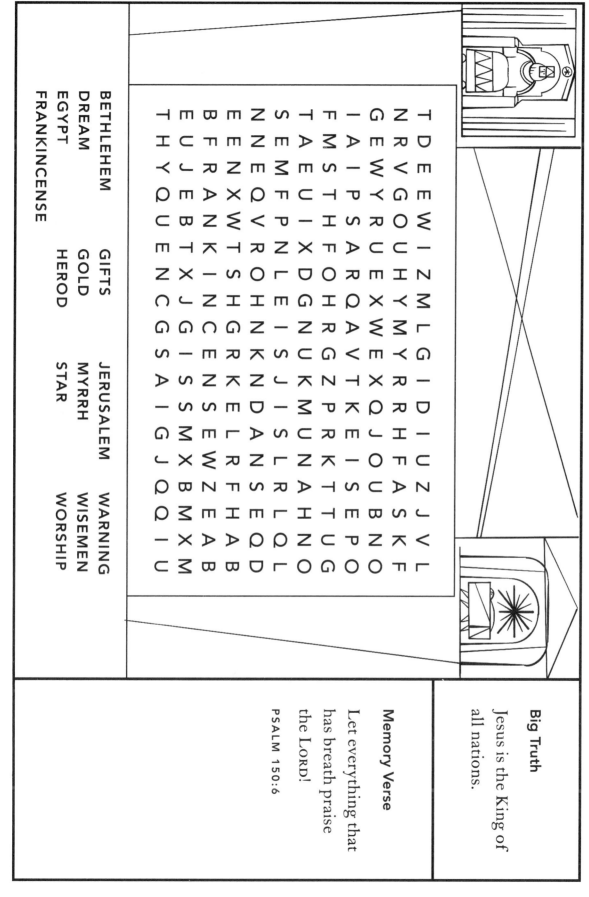

T	D	E	E	W	I	Z	M	L	G	I	D	I	U	Z	J	V	L
N	R	V	G	O	U	H	Y	M	Y	R	R	H	F	A	S	K	F
G	E	W	Y	R	U	E	X	W	E	X	Q	J	O	U	B	N	O
I	A	I	P	S	A	R	Q	A	V	T	K	E	I	S	E	P	O
F	M	S	T	H	F	O	H	R	G	Z	P	R	K	T	U	G	U
T	A	E	U	I	X	D	G	N	U	K	M	U	N	A	H	N	O
S	E	M	F	P	N	L	E	I	S	J	I	S	L	R	L	Q	L
N	N	E	Q	V	R	O	H	N	K	N	D	A	N	S	E	Q	D
E	E	N	X	W	T	S	H	G	R	K	E	L	R	F	H	A	B
B	F	R	A	N	K	I	N	C	E	N	S	E	W	Z	E	A	B
E	U	J	E	B	T	X	J	G	I	S	S	M	X	B	X	M	U
T	H	Y	Q	U	E	N	C	G	S	A	I	G	J	Q	Q	I	U

BETHLEHEM	GIFTS	JERUSALEM	WARNING
DREAM	GOLD	MYRRH	WISEMEN
EGYPT	HEROD	STAR	WORSHIP
FRANKINCENSE			

Big Truth

Jesus is the King of all nations.

Memory Verse

Let everything that has breath praise the LORD!

PSALM 150:6

Story 54 • Matthew 2 • Wise Men, Smart Move

The Pointer and the Point

Big Truth

John the Baptist pointed to the point of the Biggest Story— Jesus.

Memory Verse

Repent and believe in the gospel.

MARK 1:15

Matthew 3:1–3 (ESV)

In those days John the (1)_____ came preaching in the wilderness of Judea, "(5)_____, for the kingdom of heaven is at hand." For this is he who was spoken of by the (6)_____ Isaiah when he said,

"The voice of one crying in the (4)_____:

'(3)_____ the way of the Lord;

make his paths (2)_____.'"

Story 55 • Matthew 3 • The Pointer and the Point

The Sin That Wasn't

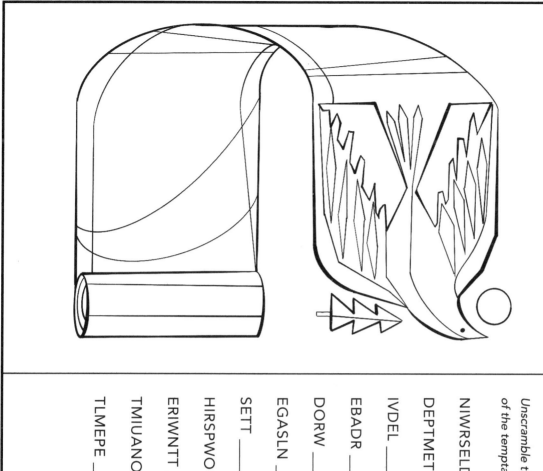

Unscramble the words below, from the story
of the temptation of Jesus in Matthew 4 (ESV).

NIWRSELDSE _____

DEPTMET _____

IVDEL _____

EBADR _____

DORW _____

EGASLN _____

SETT _____

HIRSPWO _____

ERIWNTT _____

TMIUANON _____

TLMEPE _____

Big Truth

Jesus resisted
Satan's temptation
through the word
of God.

Memory Verse

You shall worship
the Lord your God
and him only shall
you serve.

MATTHEW 4:10

The Sermon That Was

Fill in the blanks using the words in the box below, from the Sermon on the Mount in Matthew 5 (ESV).

_____ are the _____ in spirit, for theirs is the _____ of heaven.

Blessed are those who _____, for they shall be _____.

Blessed are the _____, for they shall inherit the earth.

Blessed are those who _____ and thirst for righteousness, for they shall be satisfied.

Blessed are the _____, for they shall receive mercy.

Blessed are the _____ in heart, for they shall see God.

Blessed are the _____, for they shall be called sons of God.

Blessed are those who are persecuted for _____ sake, for theirs is the kingdom of heaven.

Blessed are you when others revile you and _____ you and utter all kinds of evil against you falsely on _____ account.

BLESSED	MERCIFUL	PERSECUTE
COMFORTED	MOURN	POOR
HUNGER	MY	PURE
KINGDOM	PEACEMAKERS	RIGHTEOUSNESS'
MEEK		

Big Truth

Jesus proclaimed that he had come to crush the snake's rule and bring in his own kingdom.

Memory Verse

Whatever you wish that others would do to you, do also to them, for this is the Law and the Prophets.

MATTHEW 7:12

Story 57 • Matthew 5–7 • The Sermon That Was

Mr. Clean

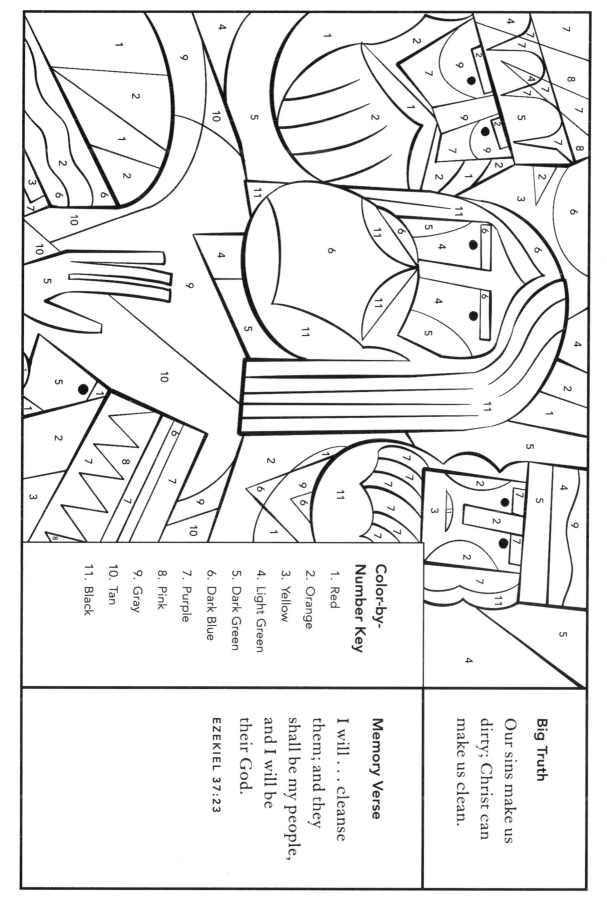

Color-by-Number Key

1. Red
2. Orange
3. Yellow
4. Light Green
5. Dark Green
6. Dark Blue
7. Purple
8. Pink
9. Gray
10. Tan
11. Black

Big Truth

Our sins make us dirty; Christ can make us clean.

Memory Verse

I will . . . cleanse them; and they shall be my people, and I will be their God.

EZEKIEL 37:23

Story 58 • Mark 1 • Mr. Clean

Get Up!

Help these men get their friend to Jesus through the rooftop.

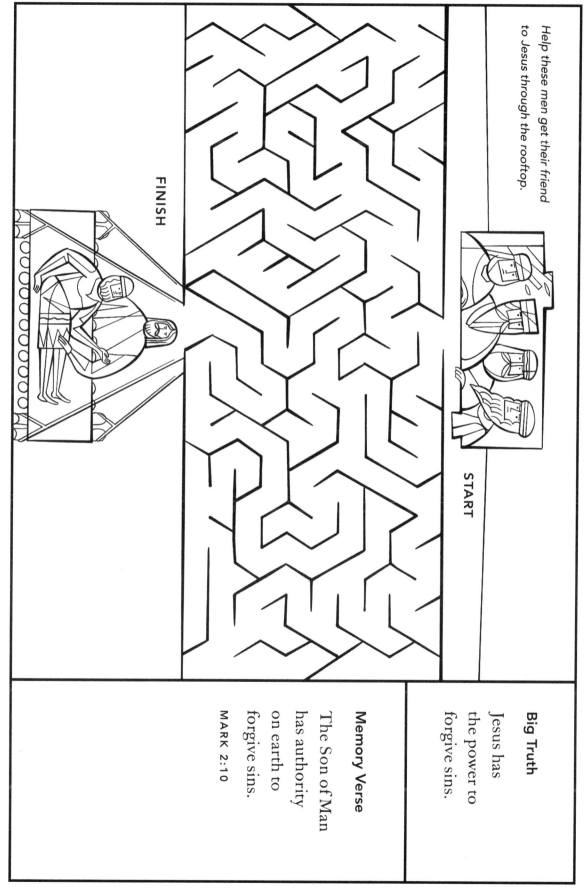

FINISH

START

Big Truth

Jesus has the power to forgive sins.

Memory Verse

The Son of Man has authority on earth to forgive sins.

MARK 2:10

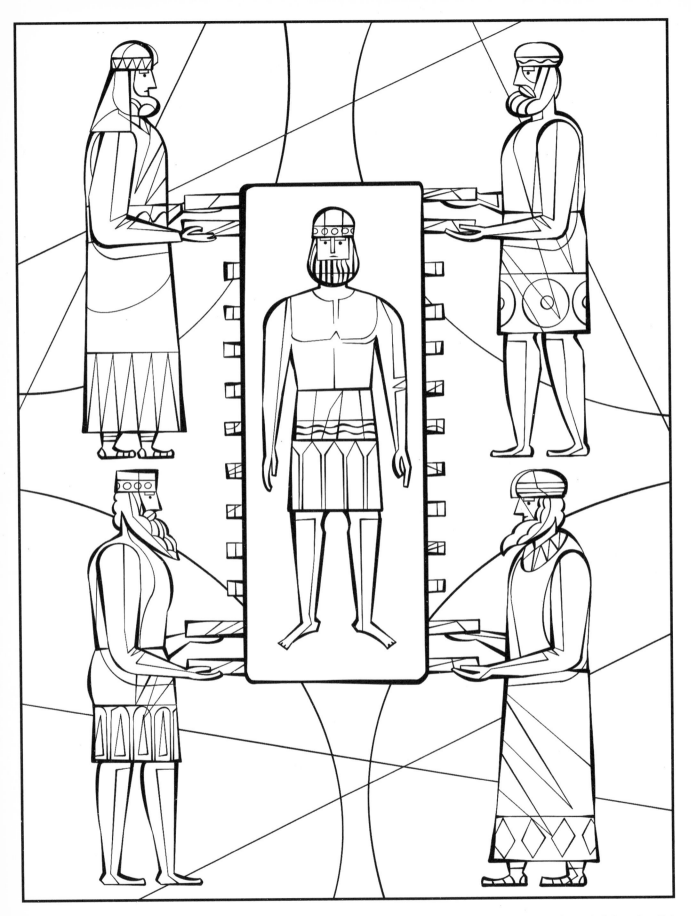

Follow the Leader

Unscramble the words below, from the story of the calling of the apostles in Mark 3 (ESV).

EERPT _____

AEJMS (BZEEEED) _____

HNJO _____

EDARWN _____

ILHIPP _____

RBLAOMTWEOH _____

THMWTAE _____

AMTHSO _____

AJEMS (HLPEASUA) _____

HUETDASAD _____

ISOMN _____

ASDUJ _____

Big Truth

Jesus picked twelve ordinary men to do extraordinary things.

Memory Verse

If anyone would come after me, let him deny himself and take up his cross and follow me.

MARK 8:34

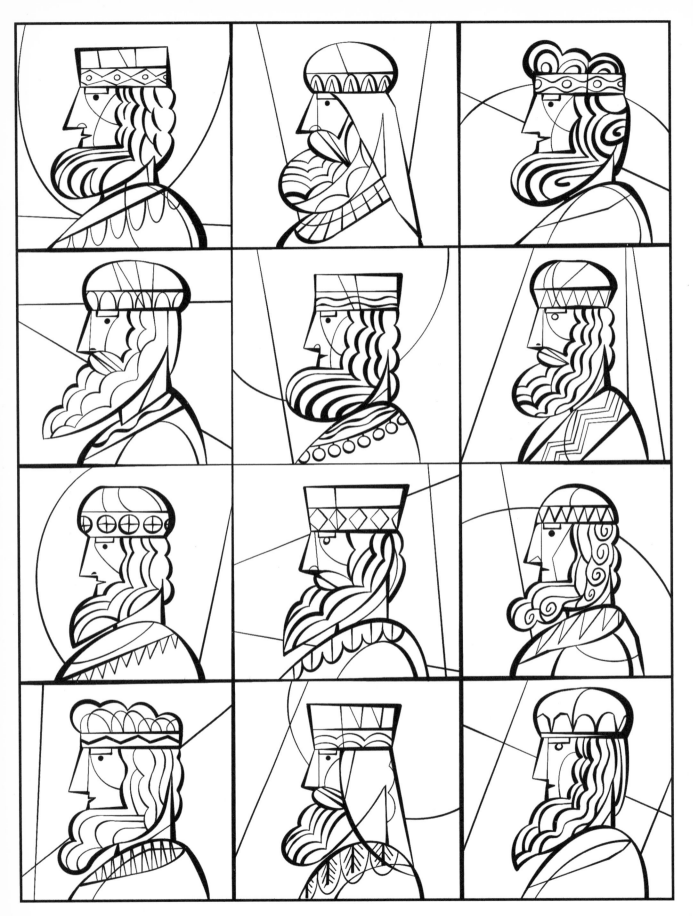

A Story about Soils

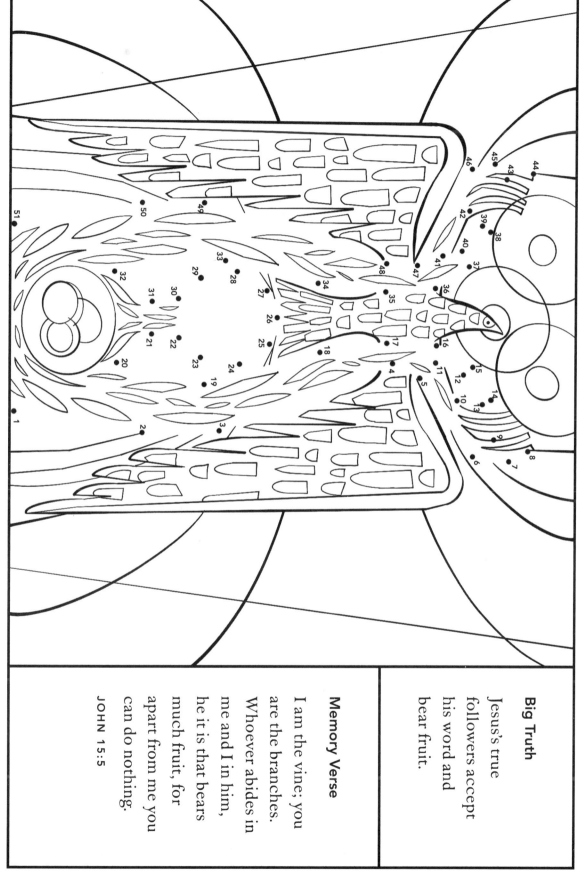

Big Truth

Jesus's true followers accept his word and bear fruit.

Memory Verse

I am the vine; you are the branches. Whoever abides in me and I in him, he it is that bears much fruit, for apart from me you can do nothing.

JOHN 15:5

The Scary Boat Ride

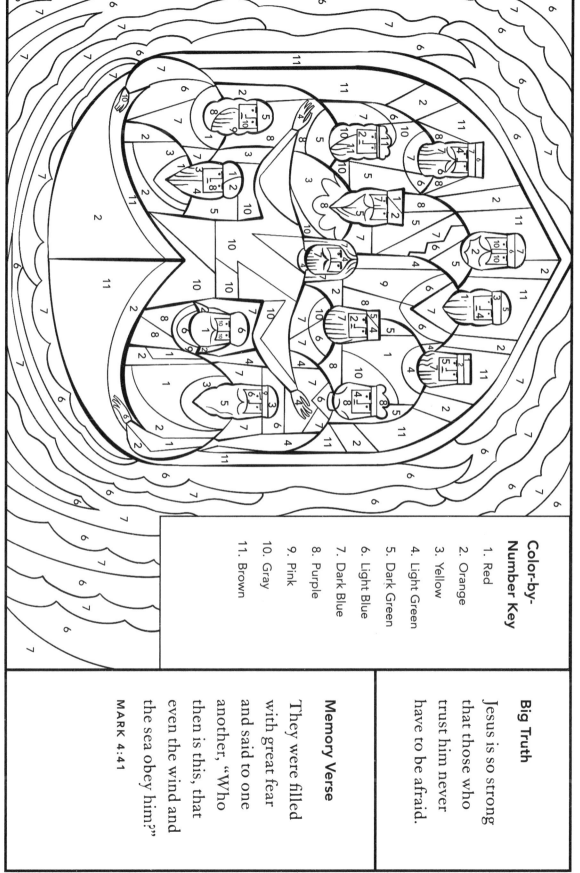

Color-by-Number Key

1. Red
2. Orange
3. Yellow
4. Light Green
5. Dark Green
6. Light Blue
7. Dark Blue
8. Purple
9. Pink
10. Gray
11. Brown

Big Truth

Jesus is so strong that those who trust him never have to be afraid.

Memory Verse

They were filled with great fear and said to one another, "Who then is this, that even the wind and the sea obey him?"

MARK 4:41

Story 62 • Mark 4 • The Scary Boat Ride

Send Us to the Pigs!

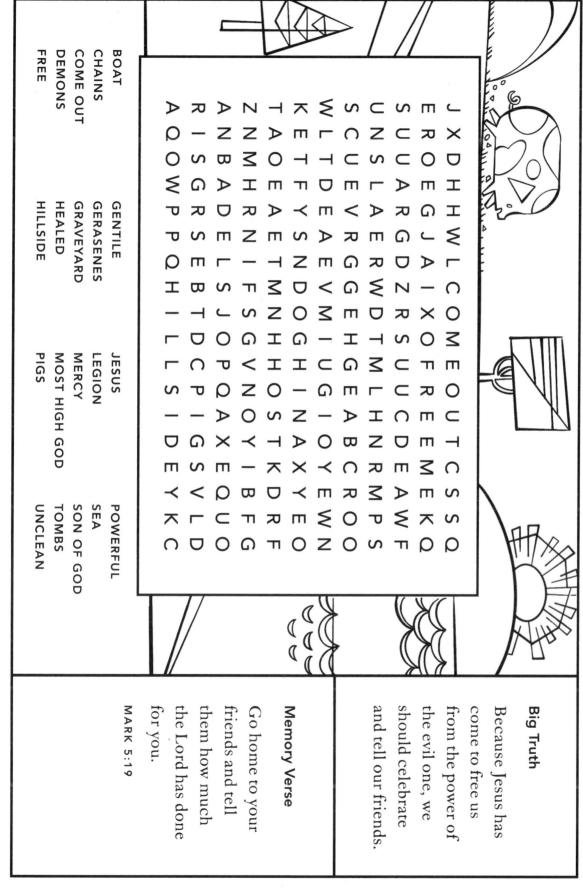

J X D H H W L C O M E O U T C S S Q
E R O E G J A I X O F R E E M E K Q
S U U A R G D Z R S U U C D E A W F
U N S L A E R W D T M L H N R M P S
S C U E V R G G E H G E A B C R O O
W L T D E A E V M I U G I O Y E W N
K E T F Y S N D O G H I N A X Y E O
T A O E A E T M N H H O S T K D R F
Z N M H R N I F S G V N O Y I B F G
A N B A D E L S J O P Q A X E Q U O
R I S G R S E B T D C P I G S V L D
A Q O W P P Q H I L L S I D E Y K C

BOAT	GENTILE	JESUS	POWERFUL
CHAINS	GERASENES	LEGION	SEA
COME OUT	GRAVEYARD	MERCY	SON OF GOD
DEMONS	HEALED	MOST HIGH GOD	TOMBS
FREE	HILLSIDE	PIGS	UNCLEAN

Big Truth

Because Jesus has come to free us from the power of the evil one, we should celebrate and tell our friends.

Memory Verse

Go home to your friends and tell them how much the Lord has done for you.

MARK 5:19

A Sick Woman and a Sad Dad

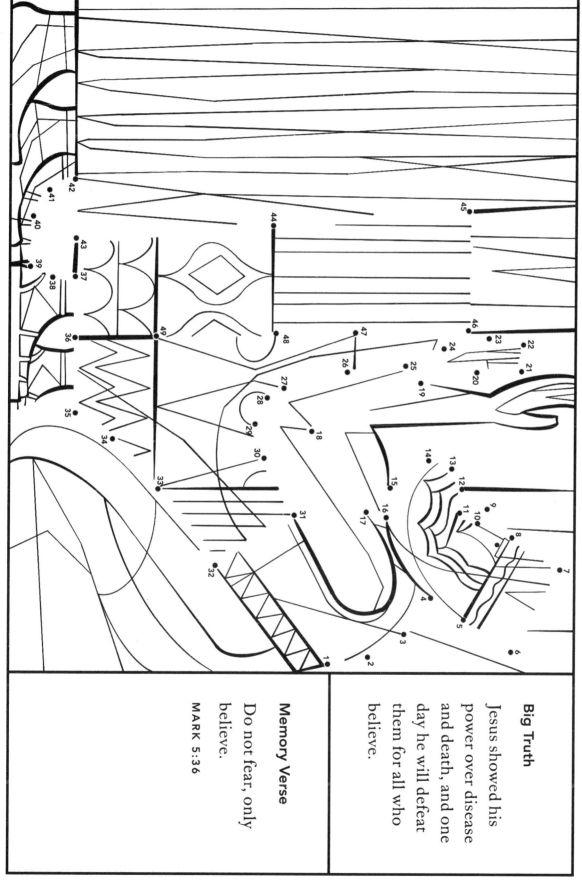

Big Truth

Jesus showed his power over disease and death, and one day he will defeat them for all who believe.

Memory Verse

Do not fear, only believe.

MARK 5:36

Story 64 • Mark 5 • A Sick Woman and a Sad Dad

The Voice Is Silenced

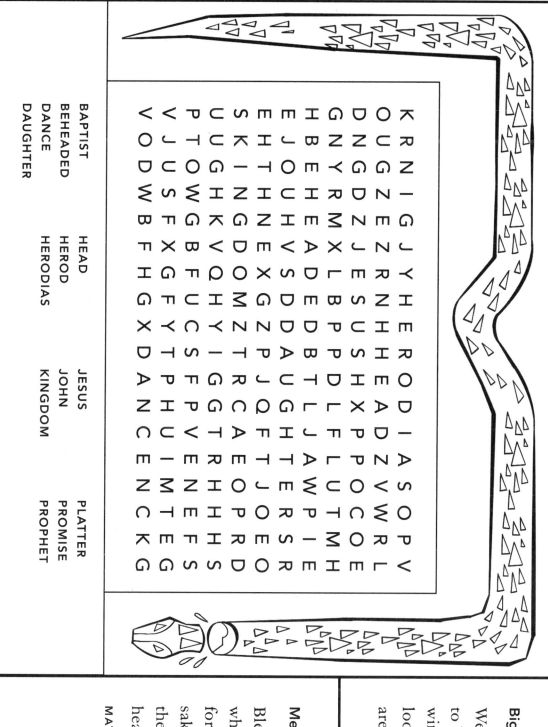

```
K R N I G J Y H E R O D I A S O P V
O U G Z E Z R N H E A D Z V W R L
D N G D Z J E S U S H X P P O C O E
G N Y R M X L B P P D L F L U T M H
H B E H E A D E D B T L J A W P I E
E J O U H V S D D A U G H T E R S R
S K I N G D O M Z T R C A E O P R D
U U G H K V Q H Y I G G T R H H S
P T O W G B F U C S F P V E N E F S
V J U S F X G F Y T P H U I M T E G
V O D W B F H G X D A N C E N C K G
```

BAPTIST	HEAD	JESUS	PLATTER
BEHEADED	HEROD	JOHN	PROMISE
DANCE	HERODIAS	KINGDOM	PROPHET
DAUGHTER			

Big Truth

We need faith to believe Jesus wins—even when it looks like bad guys are winning.

Memory Verse

Blessed are those who are persecuted for righteousness' sake, for theirs is the kingdom of heaven.

MATTHEW 5:10

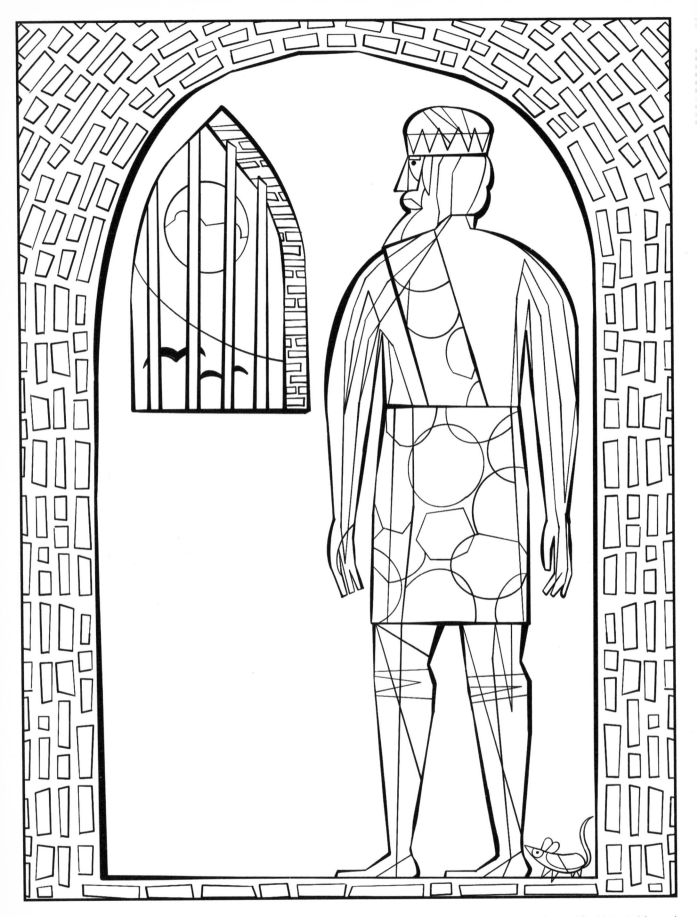

The Happy Meal That Kept on Going

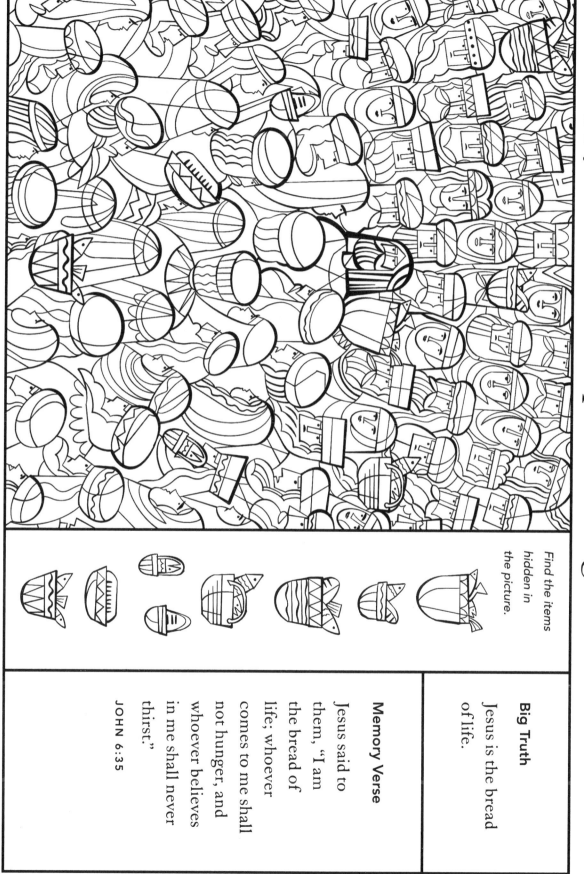

Find the items hidden in the picture.

Big Truth

Jesus is the bread of life.

Memory Verse

Jesus said to them, "I am the bread of life; whoever comes to me shall not hunger, and whoever believes in me shall never thirst."

JOHN 6:35

A Walk on the Water

Fill in the blanks using the words in the box below, from Mark 4:35–41 (ESV).

On that day, when _____ had come, he said to them, "Let us go _____ to the other side." And leaving the crowd, they took him with them in the _____, just as he was. And other boats were with him. And a great _____ arose, and the waves were breaking into the boat, so that the boat was already _____. But he was in the stern, _____ on the cushion. And they woke him and said to him, "Teacher, do you not care that we are _____?" And he awoke and _____ the wind and said to the sea, "_____! Be still!" And the wind ceased, and there was a great calm. He said to them, "Why are you so _____? Have you still no _____?" And they were filled with great _____ and said to one another, "Who then is this, that even the _____ and the sea obey him?"

ACROSS	FAITH	PERISHING
AFRAID	FEAR	REBUKED
ASLEEP	FILLING	WIND
BOAT	PEACE	WINDSTORM
EVENING		

Big Truth

Because Jesus is the Son of God, he can save us when we cry out to him.

Memory Verse

Truly you are the Son of God.

MATTHEW 14:33

A Dogged Faith

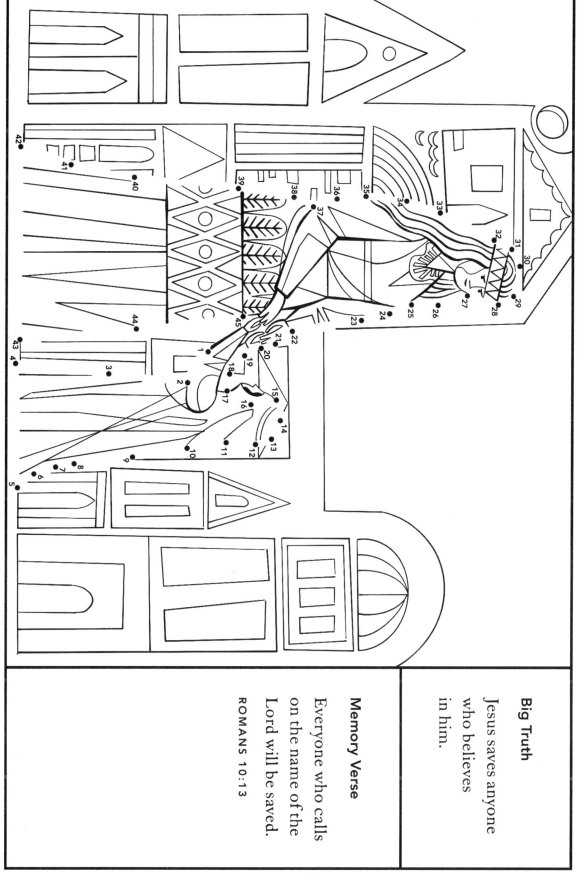

Big Truth

Jesus saves anyone who believes in him.

Memory Verse

Everyone who calls on the name of the Lord will be saved.

ROMANS 10:13

Confessing Christ

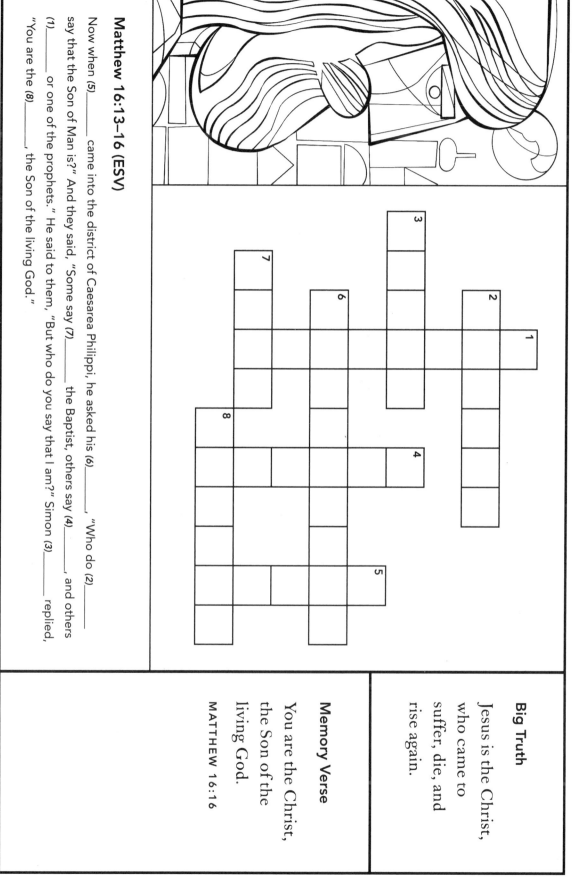

Big Truth

Jesus is the Christ, who came to suffer, die, and rise again.

Memory Verse

You are the Christ, the Son of the living God.

MATTHEW 16:16

Matthew 16:13–16 (ESV)

Now when (5) _____ came into the district of Caesarea Philippi, he asked his (6) _____, "Who do (2) _____ say that the Son of Man is?" And they said, "Some say (7) _____ the Baptist, others say (4) _____, and others (1) _____ or one of the prophets." He said to them, "But who do you say that I am?" Simon (3) _____ replied, "You are the (8) _____, the Son of the living God."

Story 69 • Matthew 16 • Confessing Christ

Glory Mountain

Color-by-Number Key

1. Red
2. Orange
3. Yellow
4. Light Green
5. Dark Green
6. Light Blue
7. Dark Blue
8. Purple
9. Pink
10. Gray
11. Brown

Big Truth

Jesus is the glorious Son of God, who is perfectly holy.

Memory Verse

For the LORD is a great God, and a great King above all gods. In his hand are the depths of the earth; the heights of the mountains are his also.

PSALM 95:3–4

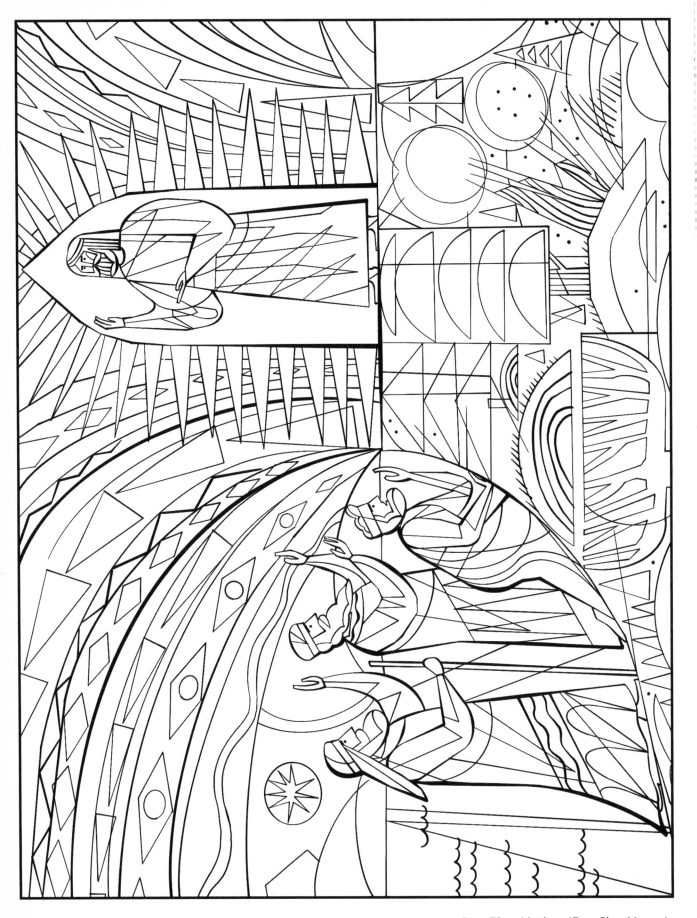

Story 70 • Matthew 17 • Glory Mountain

The Kids Can Come Too

START

FINISH

"Let the children come to me."

Big Truth

Jesus wants us to come to him like little children— needy and helpless.

Memory Verse

Truly, I say to you, whoever does not receive the kingdom of God like a child shall not enter it.

MARK 10:15

Who Is My Neighbor?

Unscramble the words below, from the parable of the good Samaritan in Luke 10 (ESV).

WERLYA _____

EACREHT _____

NBREIOGH _____

SUAELRJME _____

HRIOJEC _____

BRSBREO _____

DPITSREP _____

ETVLIE _____

ANARMTIAS _____

SINMOAOPSC _____

NENPEERKI _____

RMYEC _____

Big Truth

Loving God means loving our neighbors, which involves showing mercy to those in need.

Memory Verse

You shall love the Lord your God with all your heart and with all your soul and with all your strength and with all your mind, and your neighbor as yourself.

LUKE 10:27

Story 72 • Luke 10 • Who Is My Neighbor?

Lost and Found

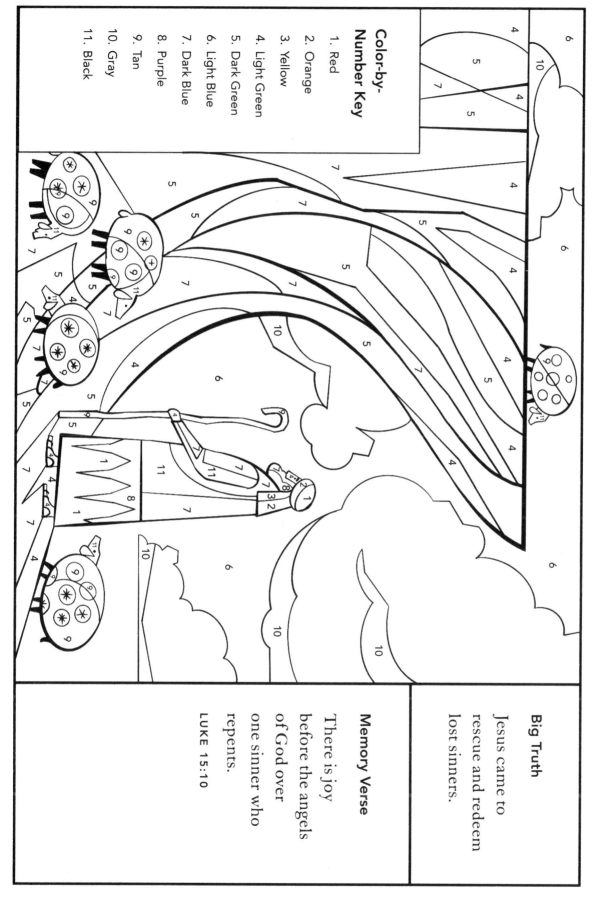

Color-by-Number Key

1. Red
2. Orange
3. Yellow
4. Light Green
5. Dark Green
6. Light Blue
7. Dark Blue
8. Purple
9. Tan
10. Gray
11. Black

Big Truth

Jesus came to rescue and redeem lost sinners.

Memory Verse

There is joy before the angels of God over one sinner who repents.

LUKE 15:10

Debts and Debtors

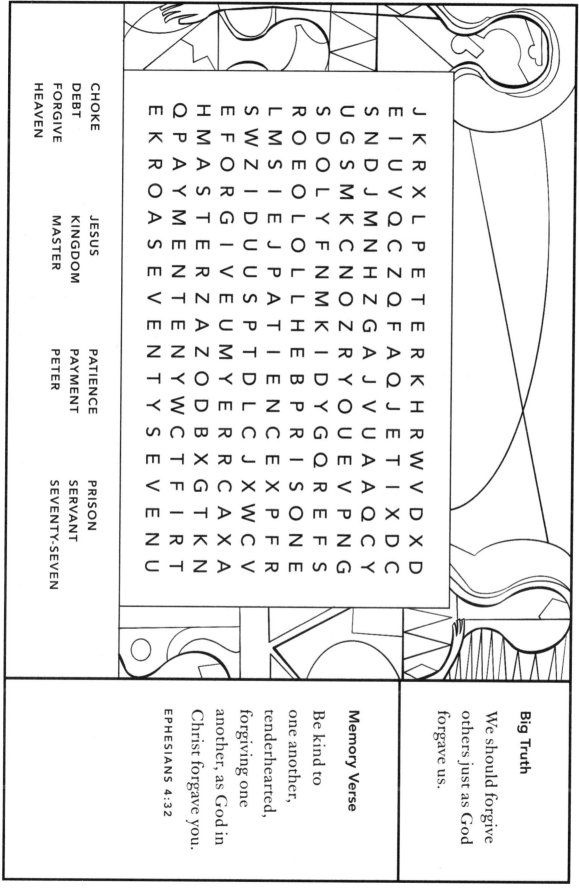

```
J K R X L P E T E R K H R W V D X D
E I U V Q C Z Q F A Q J E T I X D C
S N D J M N H Z G A J V U A Q C Y
U G S M K C N O R Y O U E V P N G
S D O L Y F N M K I D Y G Q R E F S
R O E O L O L H E B P R I S O N E
L M S I E J P A T I E N C E X P F R
S W Z I D U U S P T D L C J X W C V
E F O R G I V E U M Y E R R C A X A
H M A S T E R Z A Z O D B X G T K N
Q P A Y M E N T E N Y W C T F I R T
E K R O A S E V E N T Y S E V E N U
```

CHOKE	JESUS	PATIENCE	PRISON
DEBT	KINGDOM	PAYMENT	SERVANT
FORGIVE	MASTER	PETER	SEVENTY-SEVEN
HEAVEN			

Big Truth

We should forgive others just as God forgave us.

Memory Verse

Be kind to one another, tenderhearted, forgiving one another, as God in Christ forgave you.

EPHESIANS 4:32

Grumbles and Grace

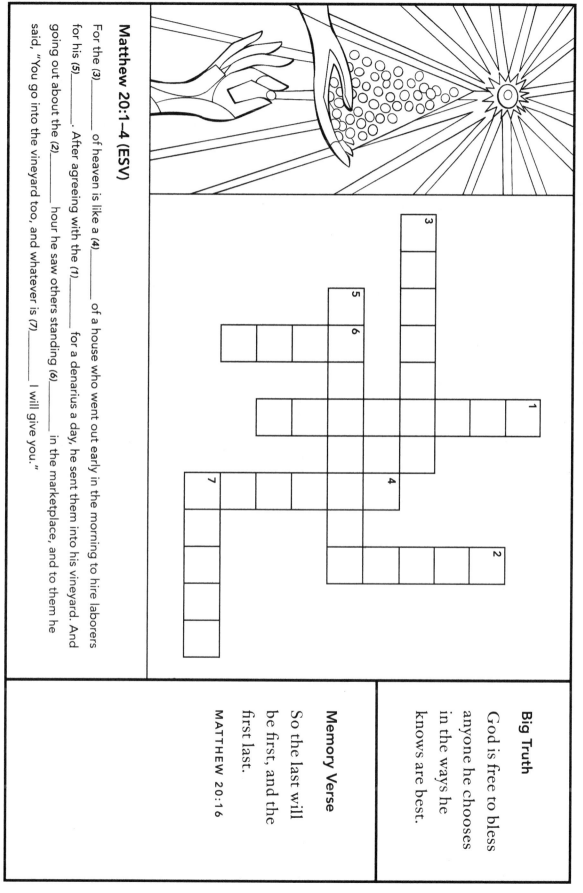

Matthew 20:1–4 (ESV)

For the (3)_____ of heaven is like a (4)_____ of a house who went out early in the morning to hire laborers for his (5)_____. After agreeing with the (1)_____ for a denarius a day, he sent them into his vineyard. And going out about the (2)_____ hour he saw others standing (6)_____ in the marketplace, and to them he said, "You go into the vineyard too, and whatever is (7)_____ I will give you."

Big Truth

God is free to bless anyone he chooses in the ways he knows are best.

Memory Verse

So the last will be first, and the first last.

MATTHEW 20:16

Little Man, Big Faith

Unscramble the words below, from the story of Zacchaeus in Luke 19 (ESV).

ROJICEH _____

HESZAUACC _____

AXT OTRCCLELO _____

LALSM _____

YOARCMSE _____

SUHOE _____

STEUG _____

NSIENR _____

OOPR _____

TSLAONIVA _____

SNO FO AMN _____

Big Truth

Jesus gives grace even to big-time sinners.

Memory Verse

The Son of Man came to seek and to save the lost.

LUKE 19:10

Story 76 • Luke 19 • Little Man, Big Faith

The King Comes

Fill in the blanks using the words in the box below, from Luke 19:36–40 (ESV).

And as he _____ along, they spread their _____ on the road. As he was drawing near— already on the way down the Mount of _____ — the whole _____ of his disciples began to _____ and praise God with a loud voice for all the _____ works that they had seen, saying, "_____ is the King who comes in the name of the Lord! _____ in heaven and glory in the highest!" And some of the _____ in the crowd said to him, "Teacher, _____ your disciples." He answered, "I tell you, if these were _____, the very _____ would cry out."

BLESSED	OLIVES	REJOICE
CLOAKS	PEACE	RODE
MIGHTY	PHARISEES	SILENT
MULTITUDE	REBUKE	STONES

Big Truth

Jesus is the King of kings—but not the king God's people expected.

Memory Verse

Blessed is the King who comes in the name of the Lord!

LUKE 19:38

Story 77 • Luke 19 • The King Comes

Jesus Cleans House

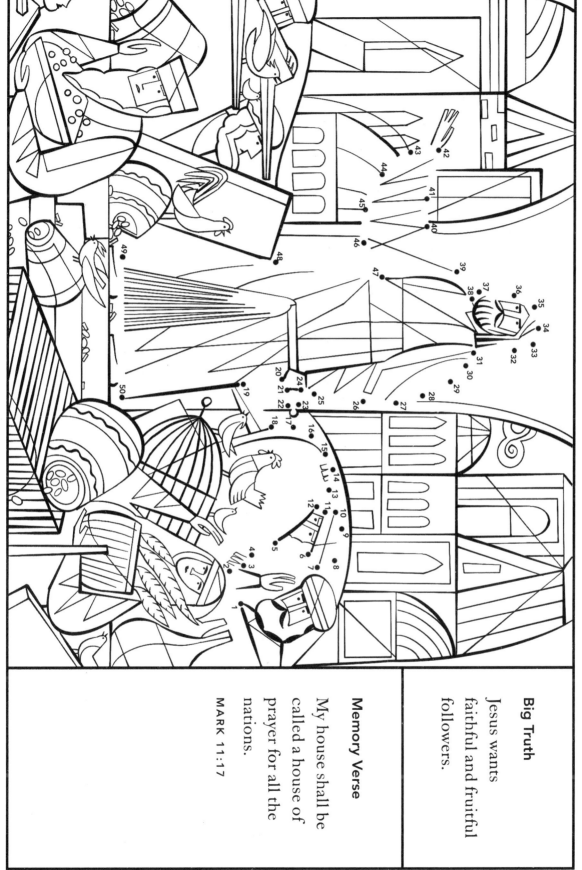

Big Truth

Jesus wants faithful and fruitful followers.

Memory Verse

My house shall be called a house of prayer for all the nations.

MARK 11:17

A Woman to Be Remembered

```
J X C I S F I L L M V P Q F T B J C
K T D Y K R V G W A O R E F I U C O
F R K F X Y M P B P Z I L R C P G N
B S P N M J M A C O X A N I F H K S
U I B E T H A N Y O Q P R T U H P
R P P U I M G N K R N X K U M E M B
I S T R V J A H A I R V W C S E M E
A O S K J B F R A G R A N C E A N D
L Z U C B O K W Y N H F L E G M M T
O Q W I P E D J U D A S Y W L B Y I
O H L L H R O Q G D I N N E R Q B B
M G J F P Y E Z K C O M R Q A S P P
```

BETHANY	FRAGRANCE	LAZARUS	PERFUME
BURIAL	HAIR	MARY	POOR
DINNER	JUDAS	OINTMENT	WIPED

Big Truth

We cannot love Jesus too much.

Memory Verse

Keep yourselves in the love of God, waiting for the mercy of our Lord Jesus Christ that leads to eternal life.

JUDE 21

A Meal for the Ages

Unscramble the words below, from the story of the Last Supper in Matthew 26 (ESV).

ELVEANDUEN _____

EAOVSSPR _____

PRREDPAE _____

ABTLE _____

ELVWTE _____

YBARET _____

RBDAE _____

OYBD _____

IENW _____

OLDBO _____

ONETACNV _____

ESRNVSFIGEO _____

Big Truth

Every time we take the bread and cup of the Lord's Supper, we celebrate that Jesus died for our sins.

Memory Verse

This is my blood of the covenant, which is poured out for many for the forgiveness of sins.

MATTHEW 26:28

Everyone Leaves Jesus

Color-by-Number Key

1. Red
2. Orange
3. Yellow
4. Light Green
5. Dark Green
6. Light Blue
7. Dark Blue
8. Purple
9. Pink
10. Black

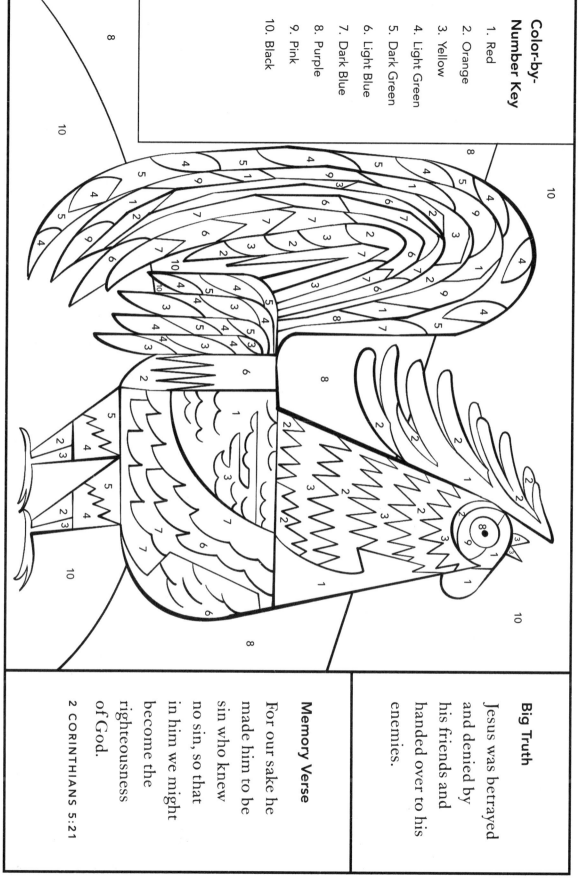

Big Truth

Jesus was betrayed and denied by his friends and handed over to his enemies.

Memory Verse

For our sake he made him to be sin who knew no sin, so that in him we might become the righteousness of God.

2 CORINTHIANS 5:21

The Snake Crusher Is Crushed for Us

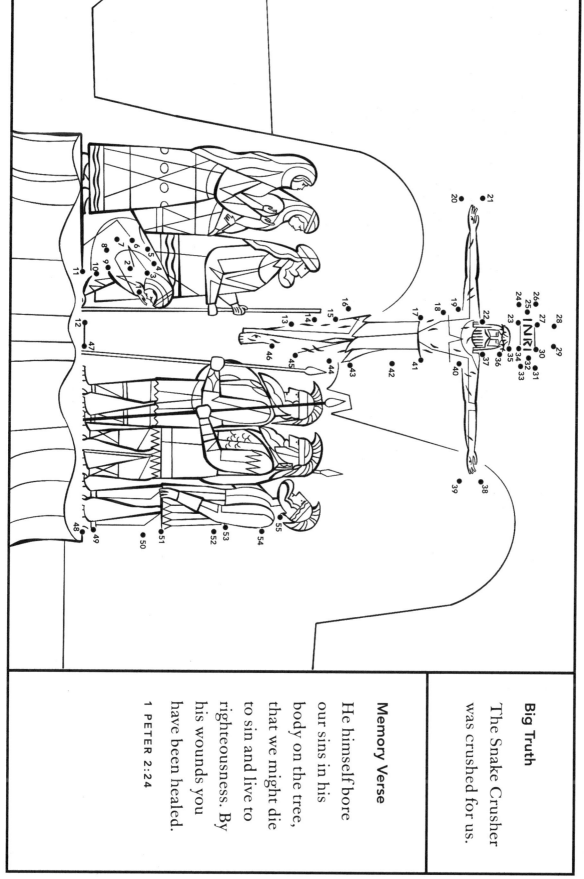

Big Truth

The Snake Crusher was crushed for us.

Memory Verse

He himself bore our sins in his body on the tree, that we might die to sin and live to righteousness. By his wounds you have been healed.

1 PETER 2:24

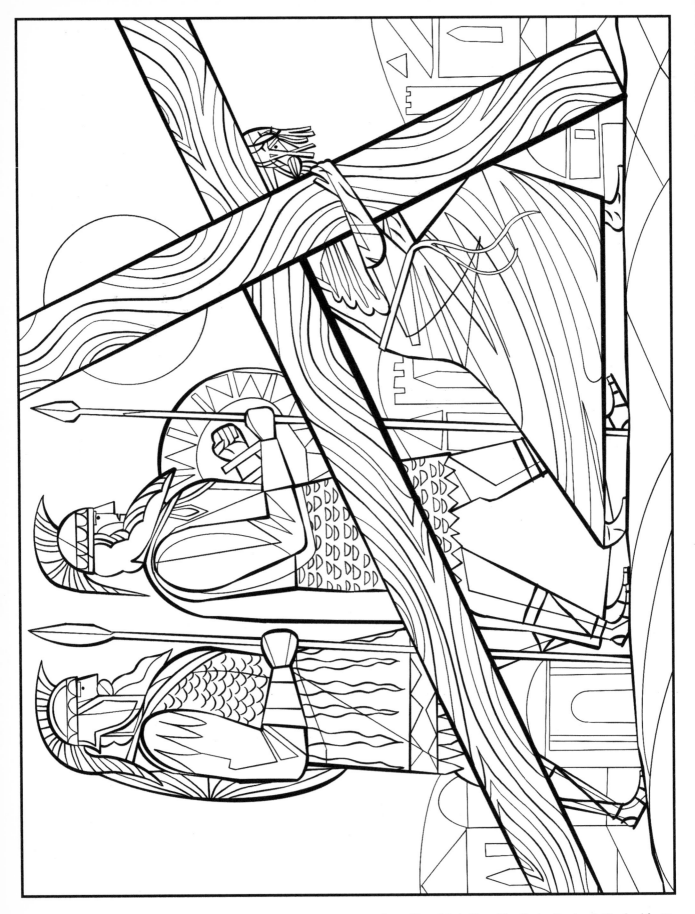

Jesus Lives

Fill in the blanks using the words in the box below, from Luke 24:1-6 (ESV).

But on the _____ day of the week, at

early _____, they went to the tomb,

taking the _____ they had prepared.

And they found the _____ rolled away

from the _____, but when they went in

they did not find the _____ of the Lord

Jesus. While they were _____ about this,

behold, two men stood by them in _____

apparel. And as they were _____

and bowed their faces to the ground, the men said

to them, "Why do you seek the _____

among the _____

_____?" He is not here, but has

_____."

BODY	FIRST	RISEN
DAWN	FRIGHTENED	SPICES
DAZZLING	LIVING	STONE
DEAD	PERPLEXED	TOMB

Big Truth

Jesus rose from the dead—just like the Old Testament said he would.

Memory Verse

Death is swallowed up in victory. O death, where is your victory? O death, where is your sting?

1 CORINTHIANS 15:54–55

Story 83 • Luke 24 • Jesus Lives

A Mission for the Ages

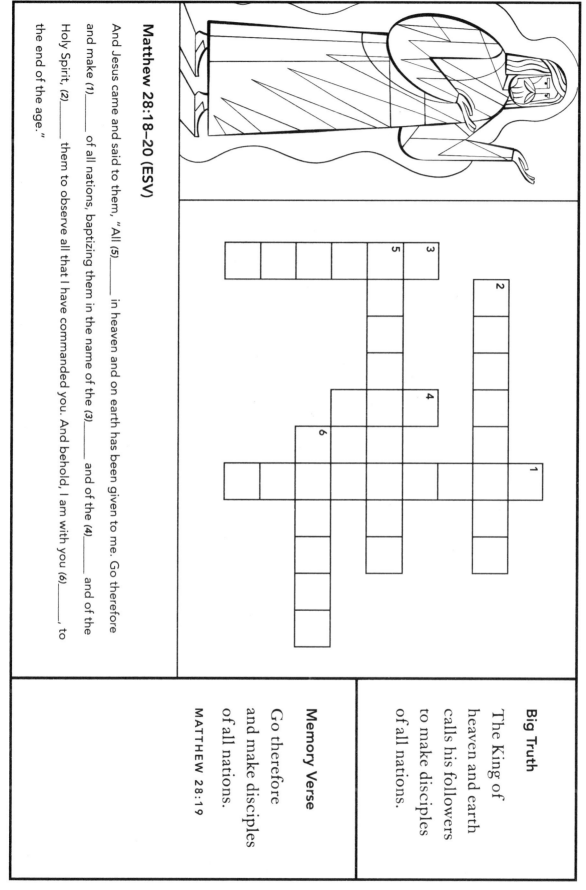

Matthew 28:18-20 (ESV)

And Jesus came and said to them, "All (5)_____ in heaven and on earth has been given to me. Go therefore and make (1)_____ of all nations, baptizing them in the name of the (3)_____ and of the (4)_____ and of the Holy Spirit, (2)_____ them to observe all that I have commanded you. And behold, I am with you (6)_____ to the end of the age."

Big Truth

The King of heaven and earth calls his followers to make disciples of all nations.

Memory Verse

Go therefore and make disciples of all nations.

MATTHEW 28:19

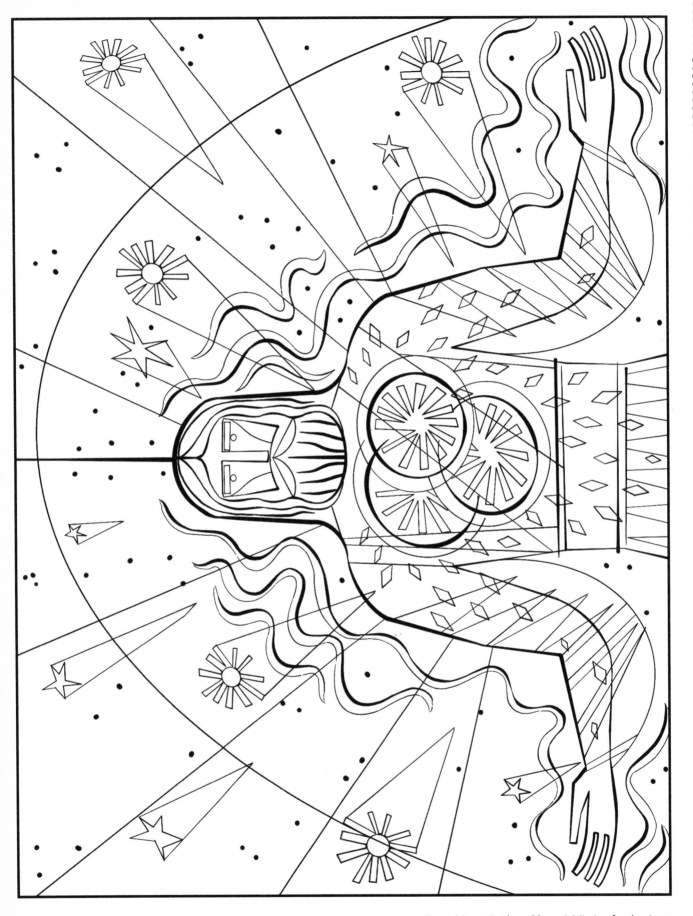

The Spirit Comes

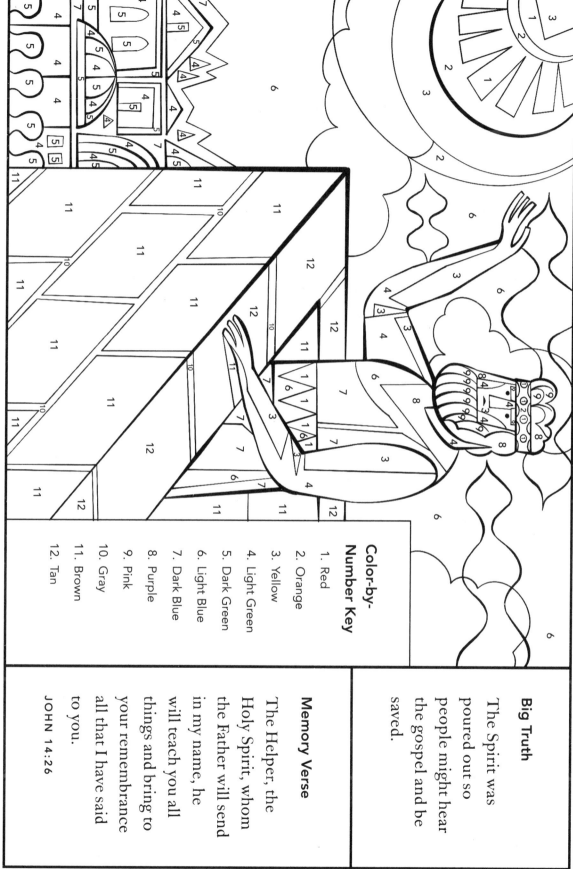

Color-by-Number Key

1. Red
2. Orange
3. Yellow
4. Light Green
5. Dark Green
6. Light Blue
7. Dark Blue
8. Purple
9. Pink
10. Gray
11. Brown
12. Tan

Big Truth

The Spirit was poured out so people might hear the gospel and be saved.

Memory Verse

The Helper, the Holy Spirit, whom the Father will send in my name, he will teach you all things and bring to your remembrance all that I have said to you.

JOHN 14:26

Story 85 • Acts 2 • The Spirit Comes

The Beautiful and the Beggar

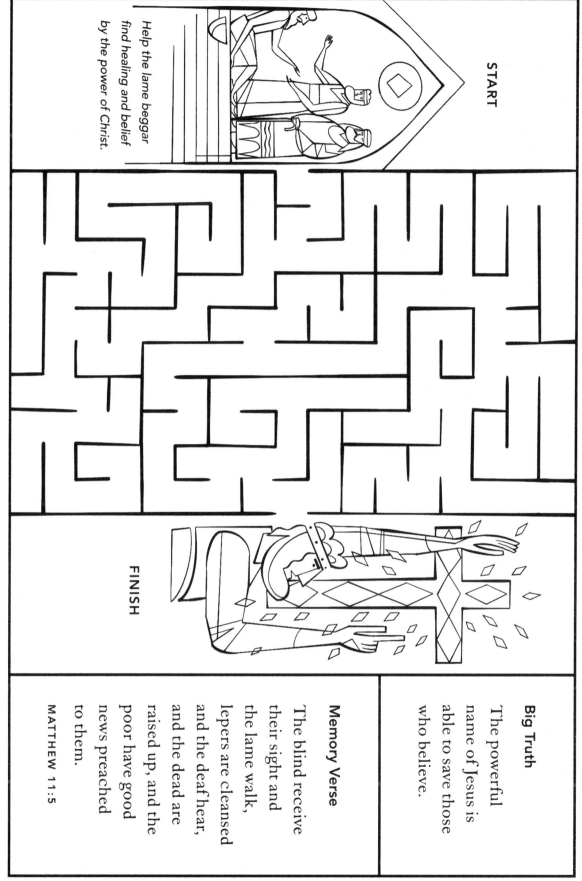

START

Help the lame beggar find healing and belief by the power of Christ.

FINISH

Big Truth

The powerful name of Jesus is able to save those who believe.

Memory Verse

The blind receive their sight and the lame walk, lepers are cleansed and the deaf hear, and the dead are raised up, and the poor have good news preached to them.

MATTHEW 11:5

Story 86 • Acts 3 • The Beautiful and the Beggar

One Name under Heaven

Fill in the blanks using the words in the box below, from Acts 4:8–12 (ESV).

Then _____, filled with the _____ Spirit, said to them, "Rulers of the people and

_____, if we are being examined today concerning a _____ deed done to a

crippled man, by what means this man has been _____, let it be known to all of you and to all

the people of Israel that by the name of _____ of Nazareth, whom you

_____, whom God _____ from the dead—by him this man is standing before

you well. This Jesus is the _____ that was rejected by you, the builders, which has become the

_____. And there is _____ in no one else, for there is no other

_____ under _____ given among men by which we must be saved."

CHRIST	HOLY	
CORNERSTONE	JESUS	
CRUCIFIED	NAME	
ELDERS	PETER	
GOOD	RAISED	
HEALED	SALVATION	
HEAVEN	STONE	

Big Truth

There is salvation in Jesus and him alone.

Memory Verse

There is salvation in no one else, for there is no other name under heaven given among men by which we must be saved.

ACTS 4:12

The Couple Who Lied and Died

Find the money
hidden in the picture.

Big Truth

It is impossible for
God to lie, so he
wants his followers
to be people of
truth.

Memory Verse

Deliver me,
O Lord, from
lying lips, from a
deceitful tongue.

PSALM 120:2

Story 88 • Acts 5 • The Couple Who Lied and Died

Stephen's Speech

Unscramble the words below, from the story of Stephen in Acts 7 (ESV).

EENTPSH _____

RESMNO _____

HABAMRA _____

OMESS _____

DDVAI _____

SRLAEI _____

AESFRHT _____

RGAENDE _____

AHEENV _____

SONDET _____

LASU _____

Big Truth

Jesus's followers boldly proclaim the gospel no matter the cost.

Memory Verse

Let us hold fast the confession of our hope without wavering, for he who promised is faithful.

HEBREWS 10:23

Philip and the Man from Africa

```
A M M S C R I P T U R E H R K E H R
P G Q P L X D W A T E R G E J T U C
S J X H U E U N U C H P B D N H R H
E E E W O B K P R O A D Z W T I Z A
U L R R S Z A V H S C A X J T O L R
T N R V U G T P O I M I S Y Z P V I
O D C G A S A I T P L X S D N I H O
H Z B F A N A Q I H U A P A F T O R
N R C K E J T L A D Z S P I N U Z N
Y P U J N G Z V E U S E T Z H A R Q
Y H W A J Z G Q F M A Y D W V R H R
F X C I U K D R D S L G H B F L S L
```

BAPTIZED	EUNUCH	JERUSALEM	SCRIPTURE
CHARIOT	GAZA	PHILIP	SERVANT
ETHIOPIAN	ISAIAH	ROAD	WATER

Big Truth

God calls his people to teach the gospel to everyone everywhere.

Memory Verse

All Scripture is breathed out by God and profitable for teaching, for reproof, for correction, and for training in righteousness, that the man of God may be complete, equipped for every good work.

2 TIMOTHY 3:16–17

Saul Sees the Light

START

Help blind Saul find his way to the house of Ananias.

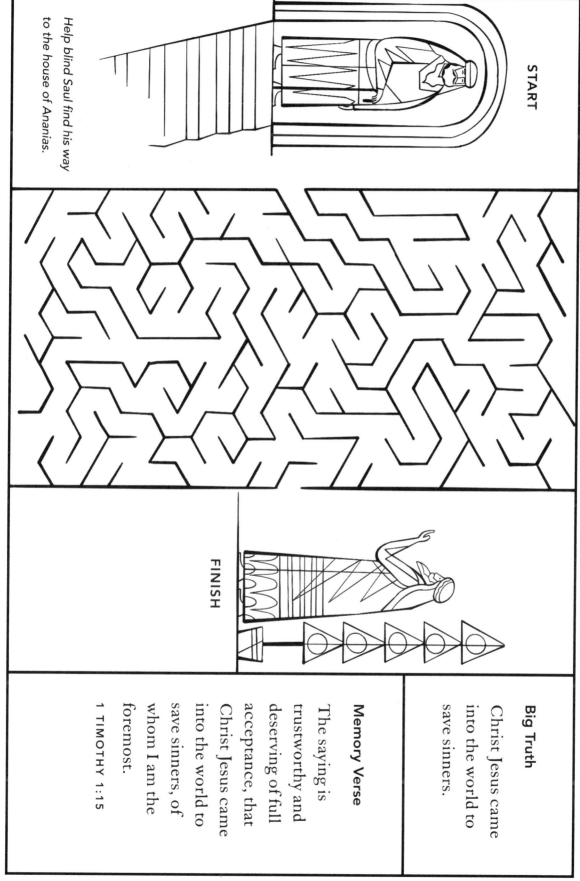

FINISH

Big Truth

Christ Jesus came into the world to save sinners.

Memory Verse

The saying is trustworthy and deserving of full acceptance, that Christ Jesus came into the world to save sinners, of whom I am the foremost.

1 TIMOTHY 1:15

Peter Eats and a Soldier Believes

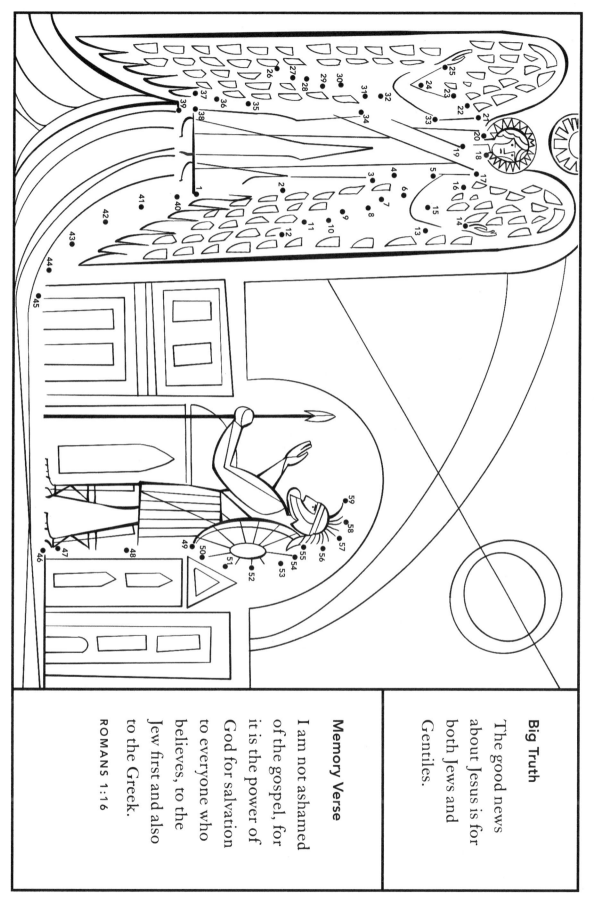

Big Truth

The good news about Jesus is for both Jews and Gentiles.

Memory Verse

I am not ashamed of the gospel, for it is the power of God for salvation to everyone who believes, to the Jew first and also to the Greek.

ROMANS 1:16

Knock Knock, Who's There?

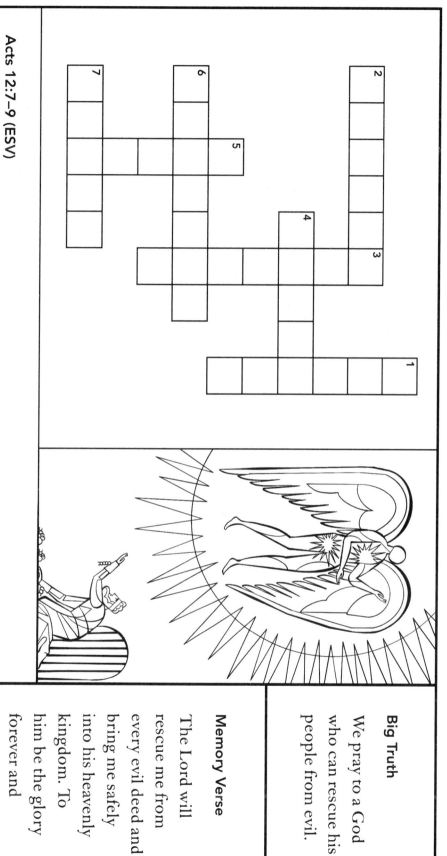

Acts 12:7-9 (ESV)

And behold, an (4)_____ of the Lord stood next to him, and a (5)_____ shone in the cell. He struck (7)_____ on the side and woke him, saying, "Get up (6)_____." And the (2)_____ fell off his hands. And the angel said to him, "Dress yourself and put on your (3)_____." And he did so. And he said to him, "Wrap your cloak around you and (1)_____ me." And he went out and followed him.

Big Truth

We pray to a God who can rescue his people from evil.

Memory Verse

The Lord will rescue me from every evil deed and bring me safely into his heavenly kingdom. To him be the glory forever and ever. Amen.

2 TIMOTHY 4:18

Story 93 • Acts 12 • Knock Knock, Who's There?

Paul, Purple Goods, and a Prison Quake

Unscramble the words below, from the story of
Paul and Silas in Acts 16 (ESV).

NISROP _____

KTSSOC _____

EARJIL _____

NRYIGPA _____

GISNGIN _____

AEKEHRTUQA _____

EODNEP _____

VDASE _____

EEEVBLI _____

SOHUDOEHL _____

AUPL _____

LSAIS _____

Big Truth

If we believe in
Jesus, we will
be saved!

Memory Verse

Believe in the Lord
Jesus, and you will
be saved.

ACTS 16:31

Paul, Purple Goods, and a Prison Quake • Acts 16 • Story 94

Story 94 • Acts 16 • Paul, Purple Goods, and a Prison Quake

The God Who Can Be Known

Fill in the blanks using the words in the box above, from Acts 17:24-27 (ESV).

The _____ who made the _____ and _____ in it, being Lord

of _____ and earth, does not live in _____ made by man, nor is he served

by human _____, as though he needed _____, since he himself gives to all

mankind life and breath and everything. And he made from one man every nation of

_____ to live on all the face of the earth, having determined allotted periods and the boundaries of their

_____ place, that they should seek God, and perhaps feel their way _____ him

and find him. Yet he is actually not _____ from each one of us.

ANYTHING	HEAVEN
DWELLING	MANKIND
EVERYTHING	TEMPLES
FAR	TOWARD
GOD	WORLD
HANDS	

Big Truth

Because the one true God can be known, we should make him known.

Memory Verse

The God who made the world and everything in it . . . does not live in temples made by man.

ACTS 17:24

Ships and Snakes and Sermons, Oh My!

Help Paul navigate the dangers of his journey toward Rome.

FINISH

START

Big Truth

The good news of God's forever kingdom will spread across the world.

Memory Verse

I can do all things through him who strengthens me.

PHILIPPIANS 4:13

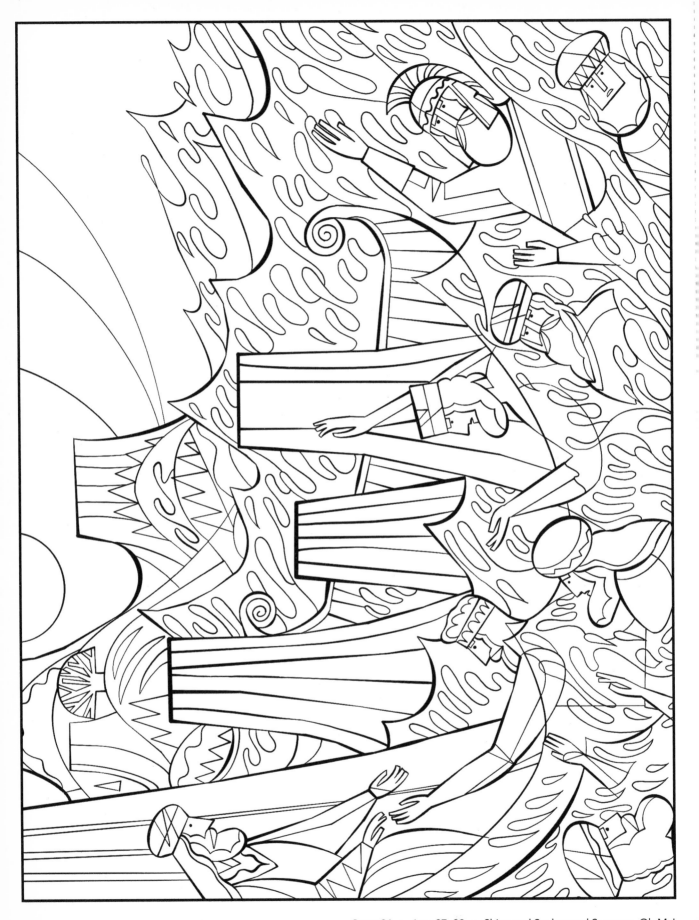

No Nothing

```
O S L C R E A T I O N V L Z Z B W F
E U A H L Z Y Q S E P A R A T E U J
G D W H K K T F B D E A T H Q J Z E
E R I G H T E O U S C K N L Q D C G
J N O C O N D E M N A T I O N R C S
V Y U S C N L G O F O V N B Z N H D
E F P L P E H L S R C T Y T I O R P
U L R A O I B I E M D H A B Q I J
N E O F U V R A H E J T G I C M S G
I S M G O L E I C A Y U I O N T T M
U H E Z B M D J T I D E N Y J G O I
J Y K H Q S I N Y P M F U O K Z R V
```

CHRIST	FREE	PAUL	SIN
CREATION	LAW	RIGHTEOUS	SPIRIT
DEATH	LOVE	ROME	NO CONDEMNATION
FLESH	NOTHING	SEPARATE	

Big Truth

In Jesus, God loves us always and forever.

Memory Verse

For I am sure that neither death nor life, . . . nor height nor depth, nor anything else in all creation, will be able to separate us from the love of God in Christ Jesus our Lord.

ROMANS 8:38–39

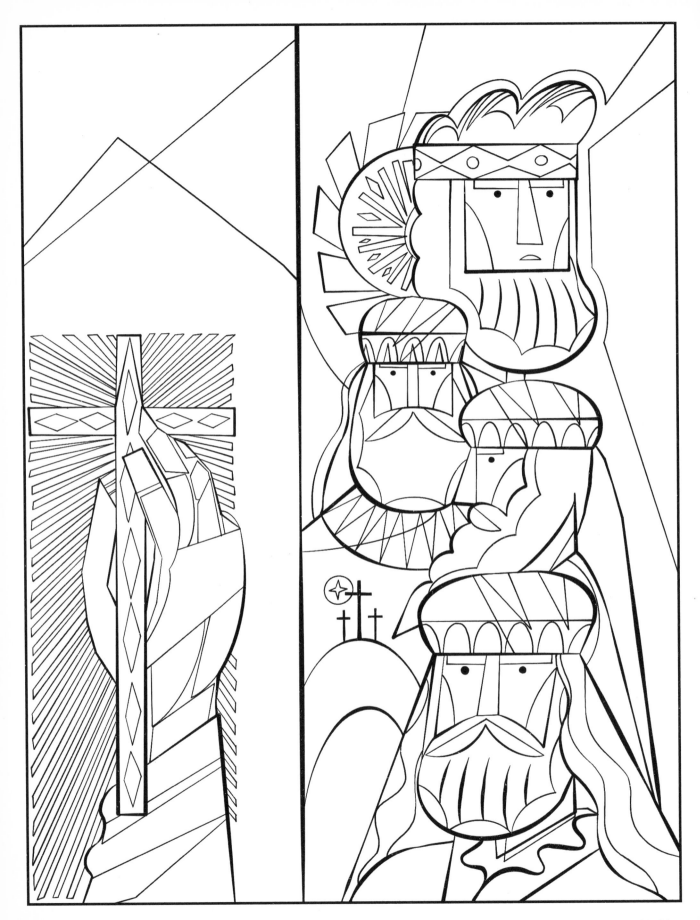

Love Is

Fill in the blanks using the words in the box below, from 1 Corinthians 13:4–8 (ESV).

Love is _____ and _____

love does not _____ or _____

_____; it is not _____

or _____. It does not insist

on its _____ way; it is not irritable or

_____; it does not rejoice at wrongdoing,

but rejoices with the _____. Love

_____ all things, _____

all things, _____ all things,

_____ all things.

never ends.

ARROGANT	KIND	
BEARS	LOVE	
BELIEVES	OWN	
BOAST	PATIENT	
ENDURES	RESENTFUL	
ENVY	RUDE	
HOPES	TRUTH	

Big Truth

We love because
God first loved us.

Memory Verse

So now faith, hope,
and love abide,
these three; but the
greatest of these
is love.

1 CORINTHIANS 13:13

More Than a Slave

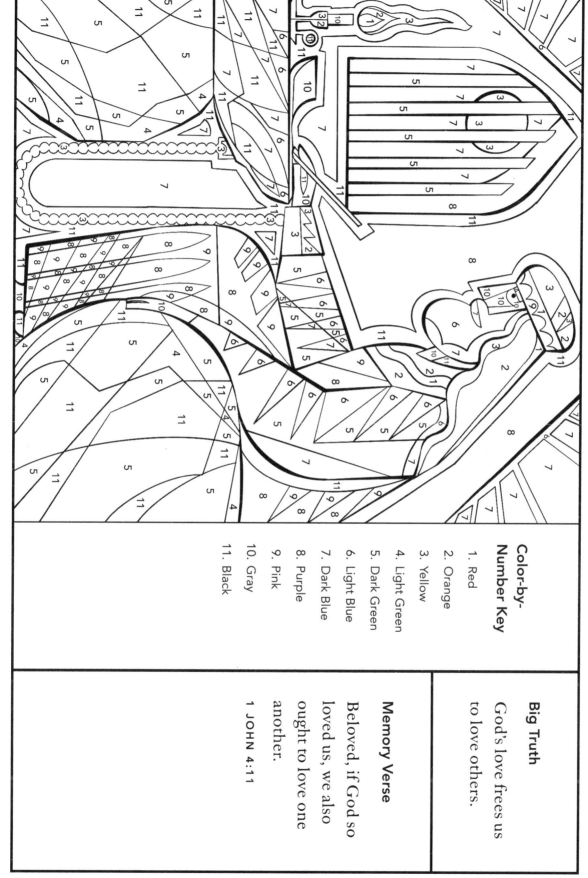

Color-by-Number Key

1. Red
2. Orange
3. Yellow
4. Light Green
5. Dark Green
6. Light Blue
7. Dark Blue
8. Purple
9. Pink
10. Gray
11. Black

Big Truth

God's love frees us to love others.

Memory Verse

Beloved, if God so loved us, we also ought to love one another.

1 JOHN 4:11

Taming the Tongue

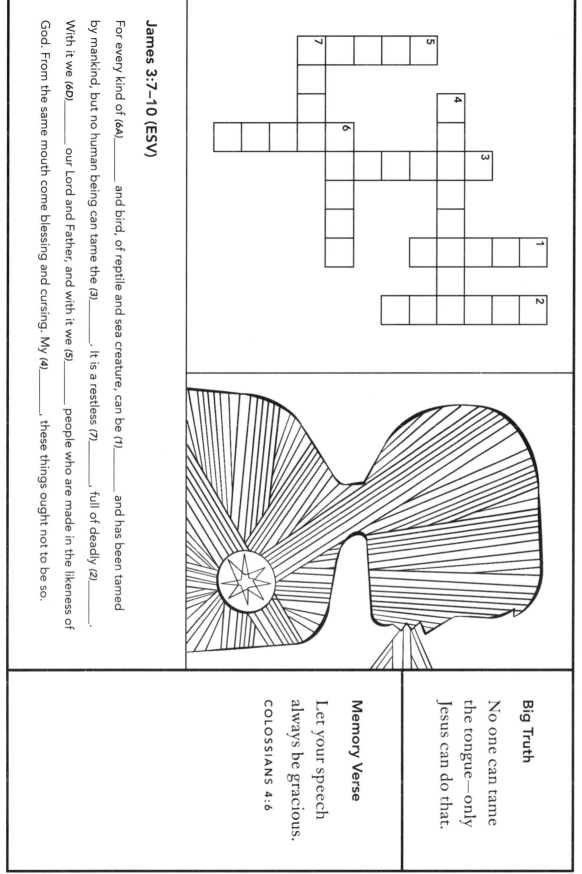

Big Truth

No one can tame
the tongue—only
Jesus can do that.

Memory Verse

Let your speech
always be gracious.

COLOSSIANS 4:6

James 3:7–10 (ESV)

For every kind of *(6A)* _____ and bird, of reptile and sea creature, can be *(1)* _____ and has been tamed by mankind, but no human being can tame the *(3)* _____. It is a restless *(7)* _____, full of deadly *(2)* _____. With it we *(6D)* _____ our Lord and Father, and with it we *(5)* _____ people who are made in the likeness of God. From the same mouth come blessing and cursing. My *(4)* _____, these things ought not to be so.

Jesus Writes a Letter

```
E F F I P O M E G A X L U R P T X I
D A C Y X O S Z Q C P I M L A S G V
X P E H R N R E N I G Z S Y T Y M S
D T T L U I J J V R Y L G Y M Y B P
B A Z E G R R E V E L A T I O N S I
V L I T W C C F R G N N B Y S N O R
M P L T B H F H C A W I T N E S S I
X H M E Q D Y J E P N Z J I F O T
G A Q R B N H C M S H G L A E I C I
C J E S U S C H R I S T E J O H N R
U Y Q L N B W J L K D I X L R H E L
Q R X Y J L A M P S T A N D V C T F
```

ALPHA	JOHN	OMEGA	SEVEN
ANGEL	LAMPSTAND	PATMOS	SPIRIT
CHURCHES	LETTER	REVELATION	WITNESS
JESUS CHRIST			

Big Truth

Jesus warns and encourages the church to keep following him.

Memory Verse

Fear not, I am the first and the last, and the living one. I died, and behold I am alive forevermore, and I have the keys of Death and Hades.

REVELATION 1:17–18

Story 101 • Revelation 1–3 • Jesus Writes a Letter

The Center of the Universe

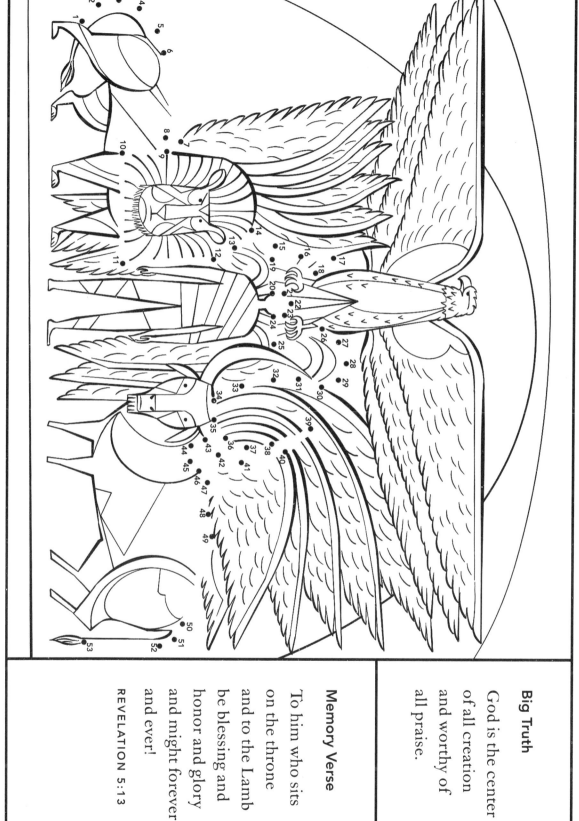

Big Truth

God is the center of all creation and worthy of all praise.

Memory Verse

To him who sits on the throne and to the Lamb be blessing and honor and glory and might forever and ever!

REVELATION 5:13

The Snake Crusher Wins

From Revelation 20:7–14 (ESV)

Then I saw a great white (7)_____ and him who was seated on it. From his presence (4)_____ and sky fled away, and no place was found for them. And I saw the (6)_____, great and small, standing before the throne, and (5)_____ were opened. Then another book was opened, which is the book of (3)_____. And the dead were (2)_____ by what was written in the books, according to what they had done. . . . Then Death and Hades were thrown into the lake of (1)_____.

Big Truth

The Snake Crusher will judge Satan once and for all.

Memory Verse

Salvation and glory and power belong to our God, for his judgments are true and just.

REVELATION 19:1–2

All Things New

START

FINISH

Walk with John through his vision of the city of God.

Big Truth

When Jesus returns, he will create new heavens and earth with no suffering, sin, or Satan.

Memory Verse

Behold, I am making all things new.

REVELATION 21:5